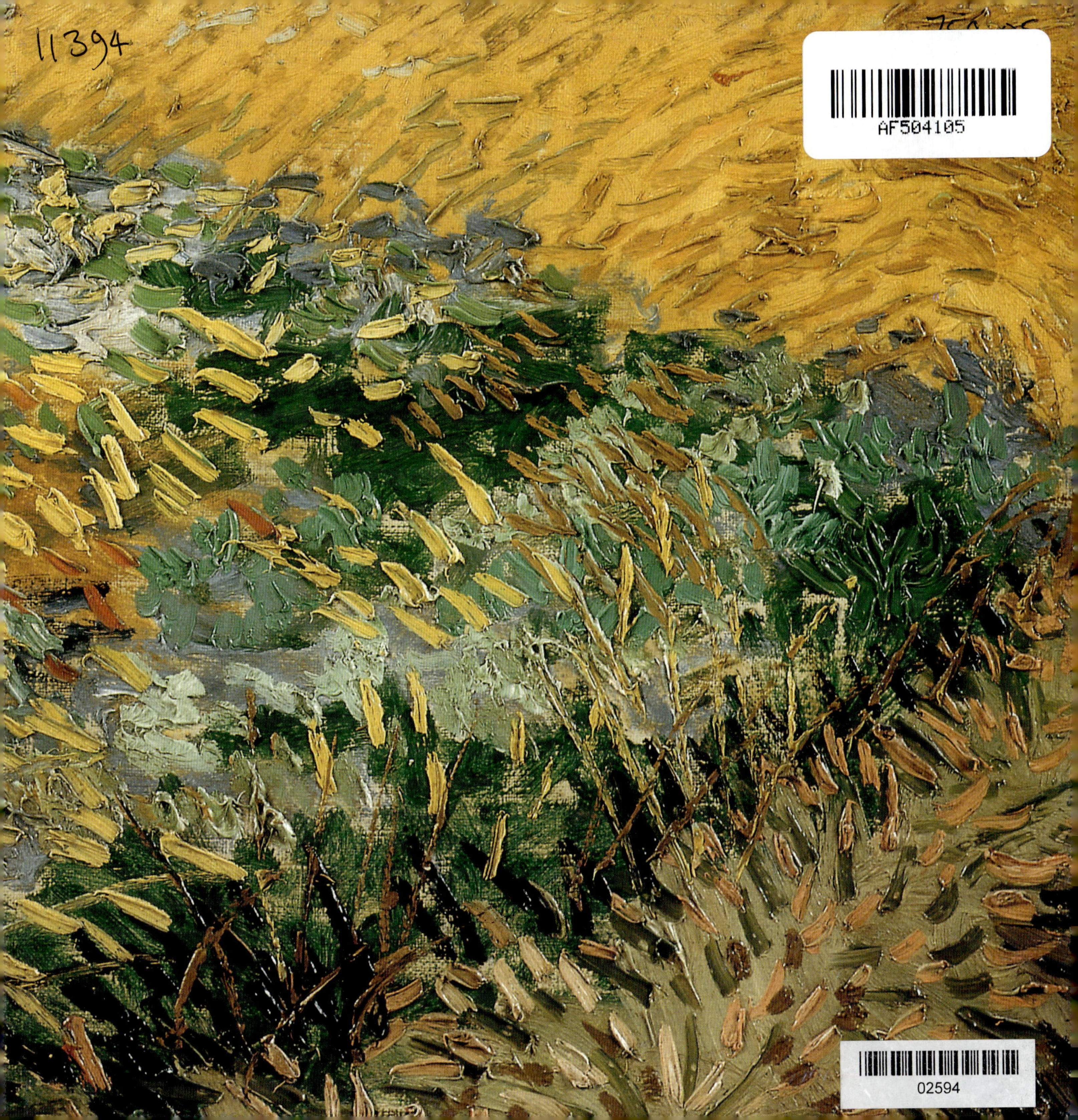

11394
AF504105
02594

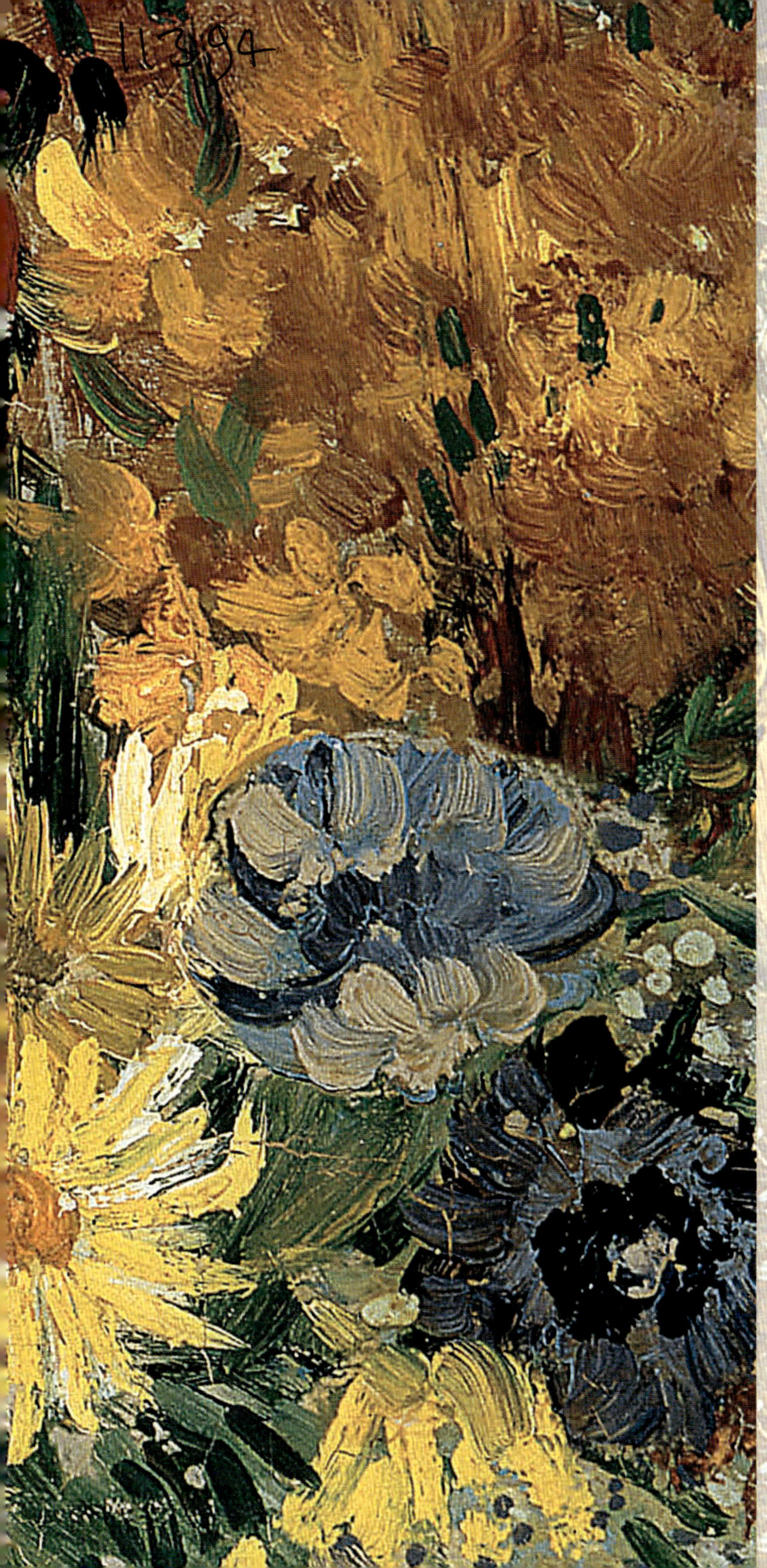

Van Gogh

Fields and Flowers

Debra N. Mancoff

CHRONICLE BOOKS

SAN FRANCISCO

Van Gogh   Fields and Flowers

First published in the United States in 1999 by Chronicle Books.

Copyright © 1999 Frances Lincoln Limited
Text copyright © 1999 Debra N. Mancoff

All rights reserved. No part of this book may be reproduced in any form without written permission from the publisher.

Printed and bound in Hong Kong

Library of Congress Cataloging-in-Publication Data available.

ISBN 0-8118-2569-8

Cover design: Liz Rico and Sarah Davies

Distributed in Canada by Raincoast Books
8680 Cambie Street
Vancouver, BC V6P 6M9

10 9 8 7 6 5 4 3 2 1

Chronicle Books
85 Second Street
San Francisco, CA 94105

www.chroniclebooks.com

"In the future my name ought to be put in the catalog as I sign it on the canvas, namely Vincent and not Van Gogh, for the simple reason that they do not know how to pronounce the latter name here."

LETTER TO THEO, SPRING 1888

RIGHT *Irises* (detail)
PRECEDING PAGES *Flowers in Blue Vase* (detail)
FRONT ENDPAPERS *Wheatfield* (detail)
BACK ENDPAPERS *Almond Blossom* (detail)

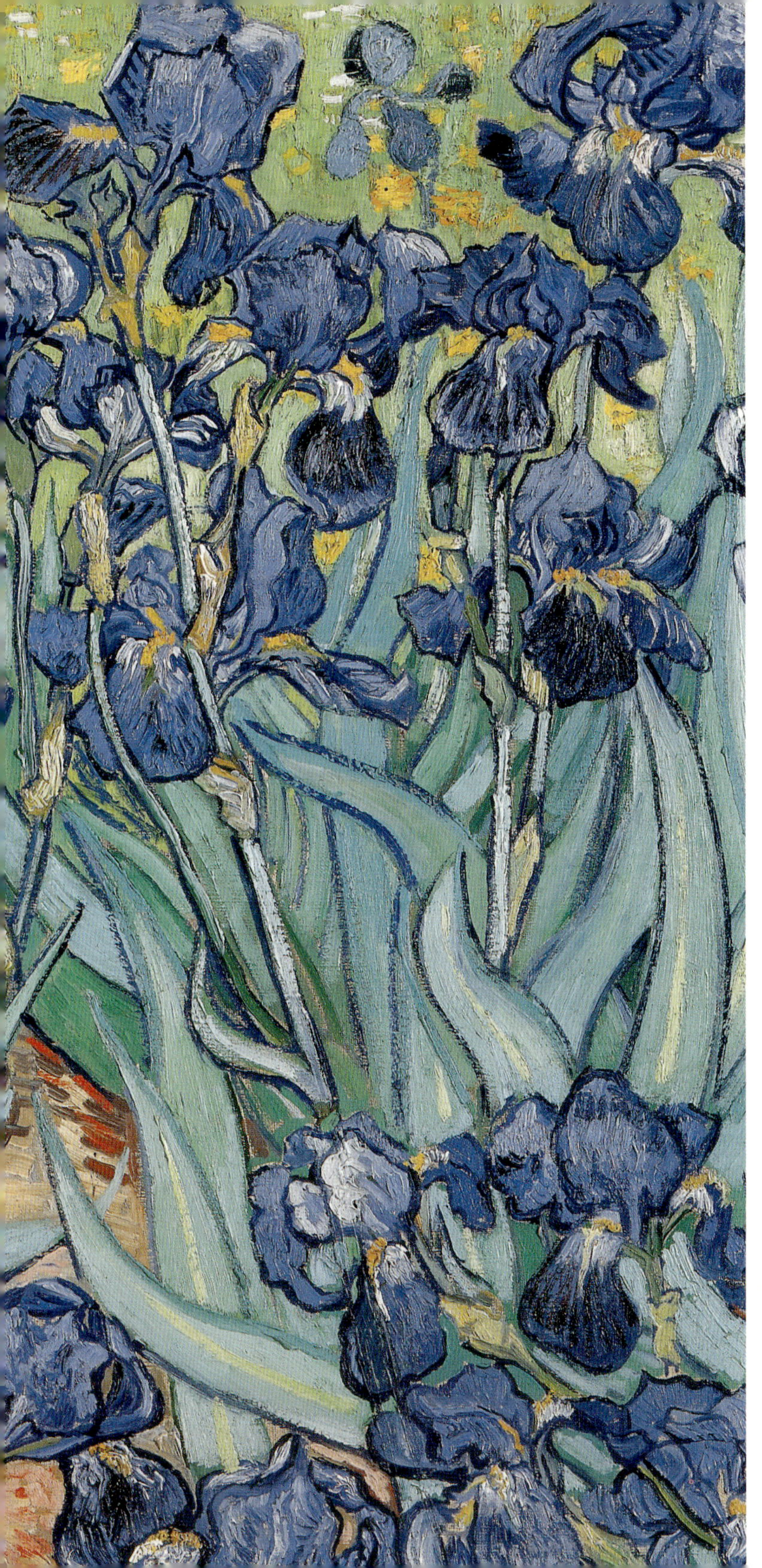

CONTENTS

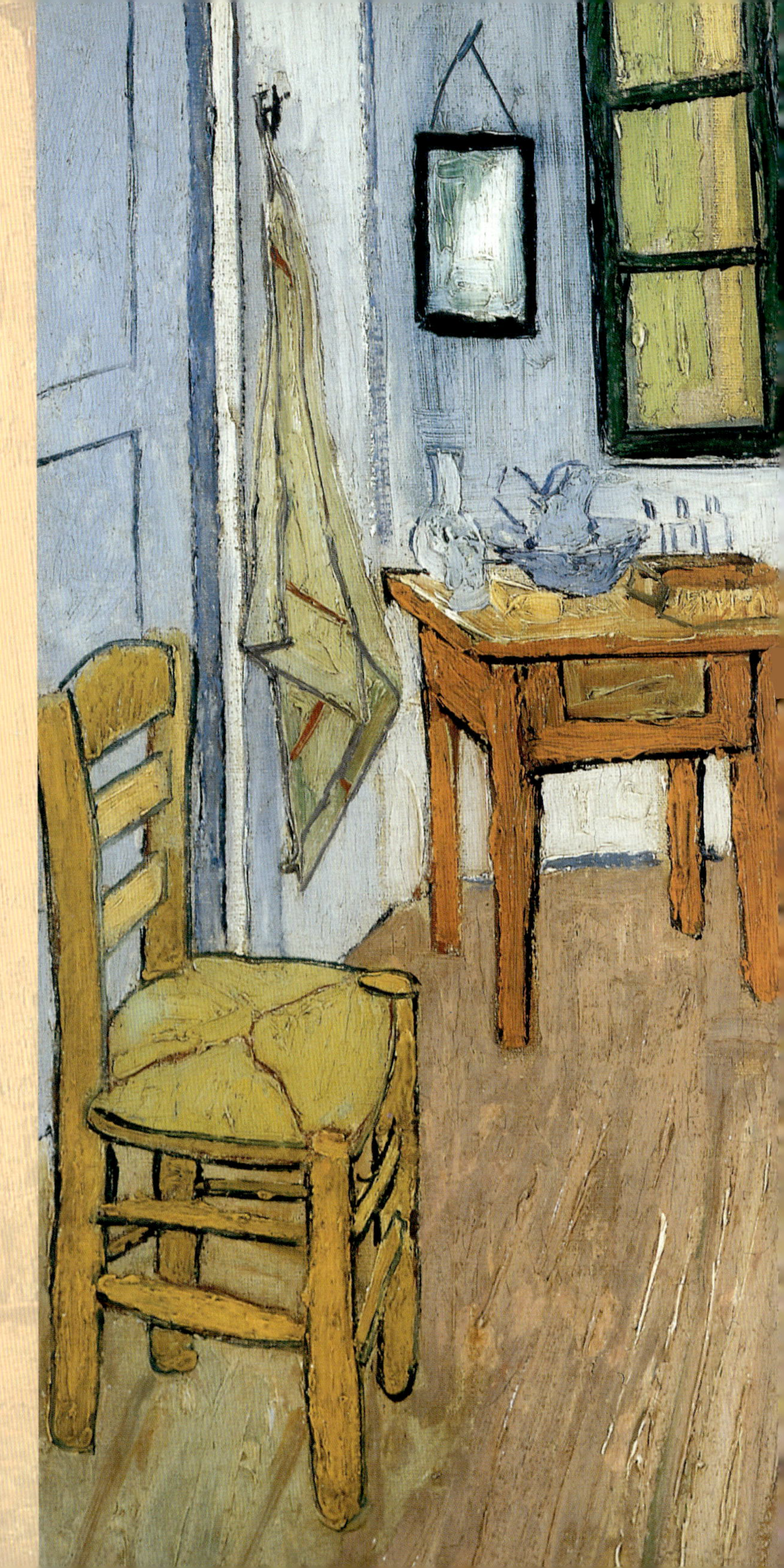

I

Vincent van Gogh: A Brief Life

"What color is in a picture, enthusiasm is in life."

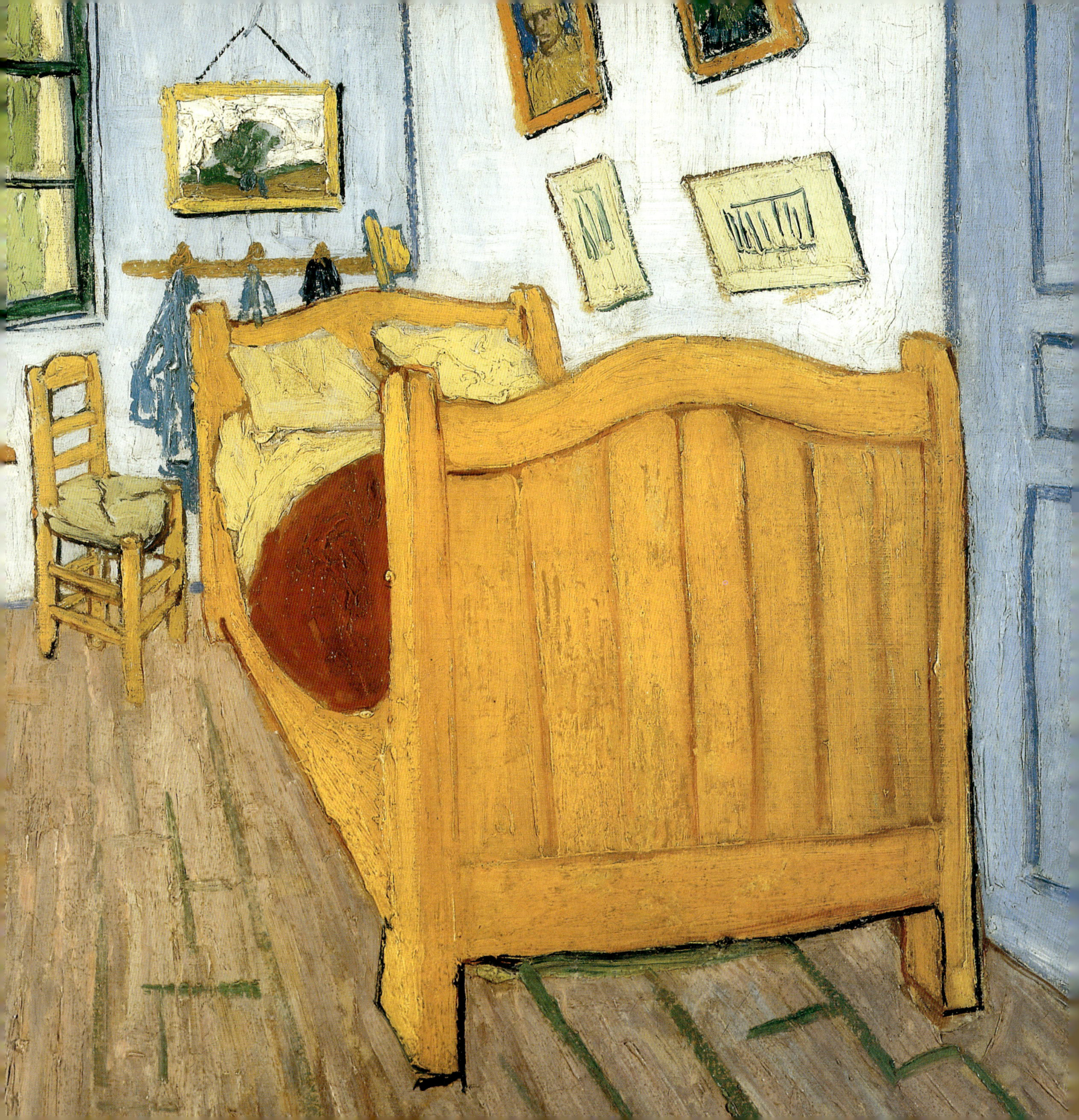

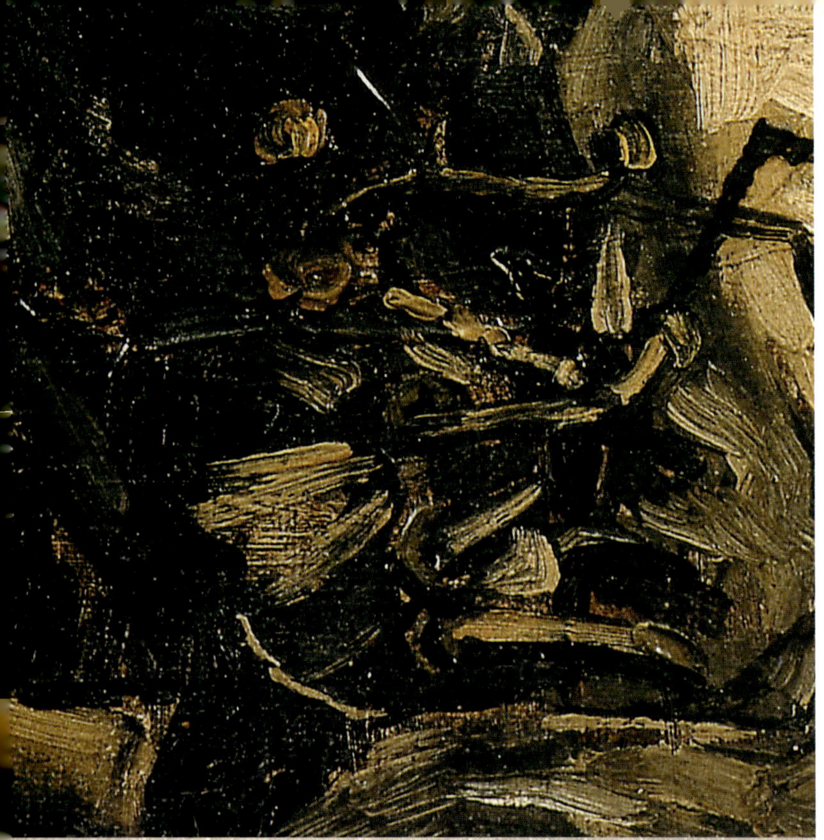

Throughout his brief but passionate life, Vincent van Gogh drew much solace from the beauty of nature. In his youth he roamed through the woods near his home, fascinated by the plants and insects. As a man Vincent believed that the countryside was a sanctuary of health, the natural rhythms of life demonstrating the restorative power of nature. He saw in nature the model for beauty, balance, and harmony in his art, explaining, "I study nature, so as not to do foolish things, to remain reasonable" (Letter 429). And in his natural subjects, such as bright bouquets, blossoming trees, favorite flowers, and verdant fields, he expressed his most personal passions. Vincent's paintings of these subjects reflect his belief in a bond between humanity and the natural world. Through them, he affirmed meaning in his life and they remain a testament to his unwavering faith in nature and in the arts.

A Pair of Shoes RIGHT AND ABOVE
LATE 1886. VAN GOGH MUSEUM, AMSTERDAM

The subject of this painting—a pair of battered work boots—reflects Vincent's interest in ordinary, well-worn objects so routinely used that they are scarcely noticed. He uses a dark palette, featuring earth tones of somber brown and ocher, heavily shadowed in black, to express the spirit of the life of the rural poor. The thickening impasto (the piling up of paint for texture) and subtle golden highlights forecast the stylistic changes associated with his work in Paris.

The Bedroom PRECEDING PAGES
OCTOBER 1888. VAN GOGH MUSEUM, AMSTERDAM

Vincent painted this portrait of his bedroom in the Yellow House at Arles while preparing for Gauguin's visit. With its acute perspective and flattened dimensions, *The Bedroom* has a jarring expressive force, but Vincent told Theo it was meant to convey a sense of rest. In a letter written to his brother about the painting, he describes the furniture of the room as rendered with "sturdy lines" to suggest the peace of "undisturbed rest."

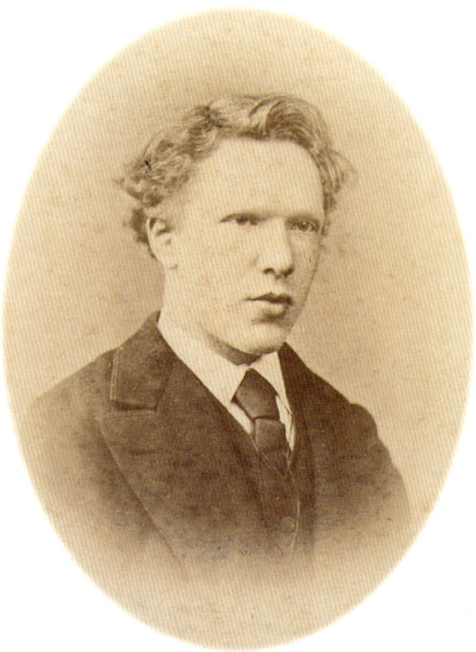

Photograph of Vincent, aged 19
VAN GOGH MUSEUM, AMSTERDAM

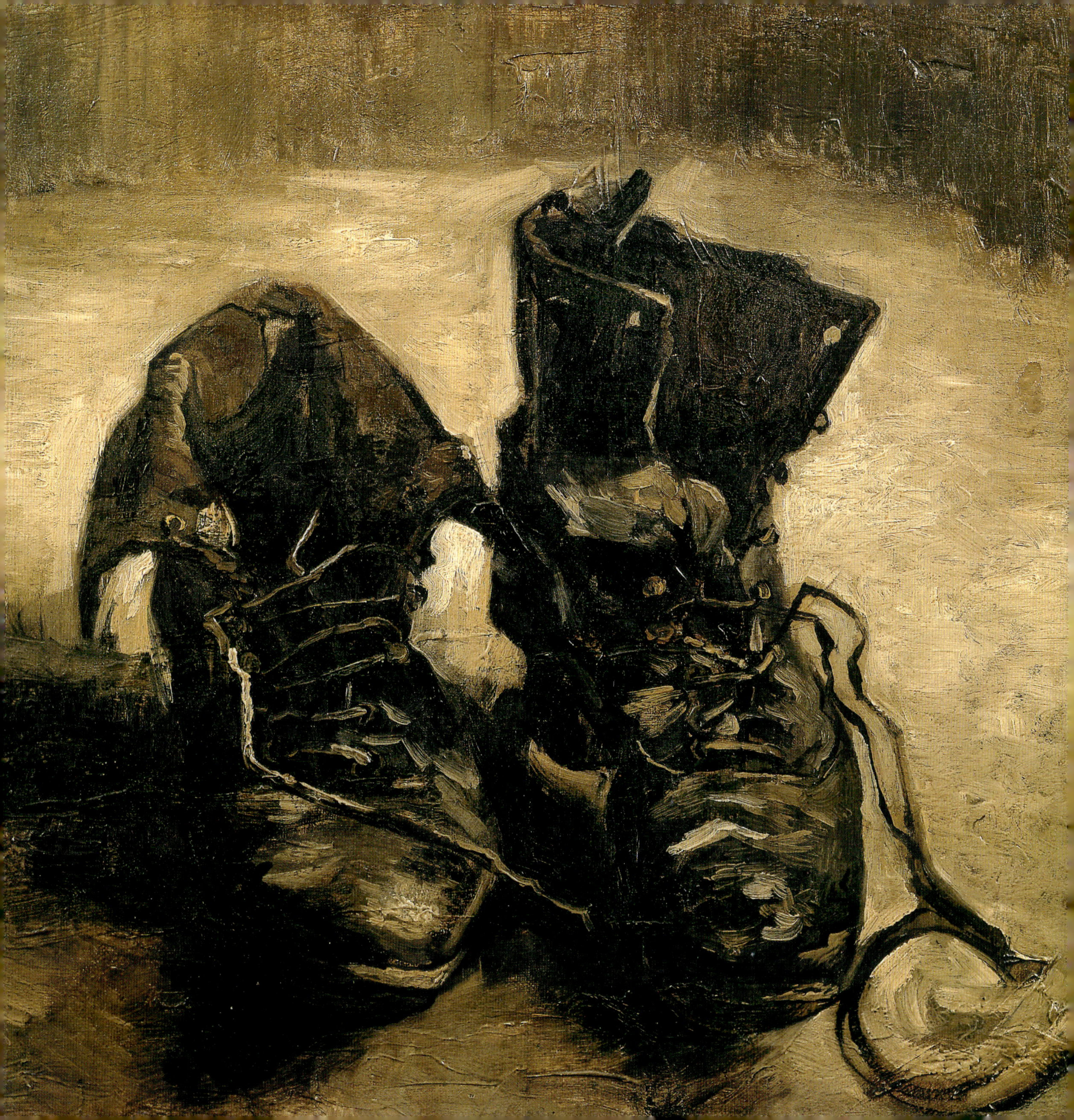

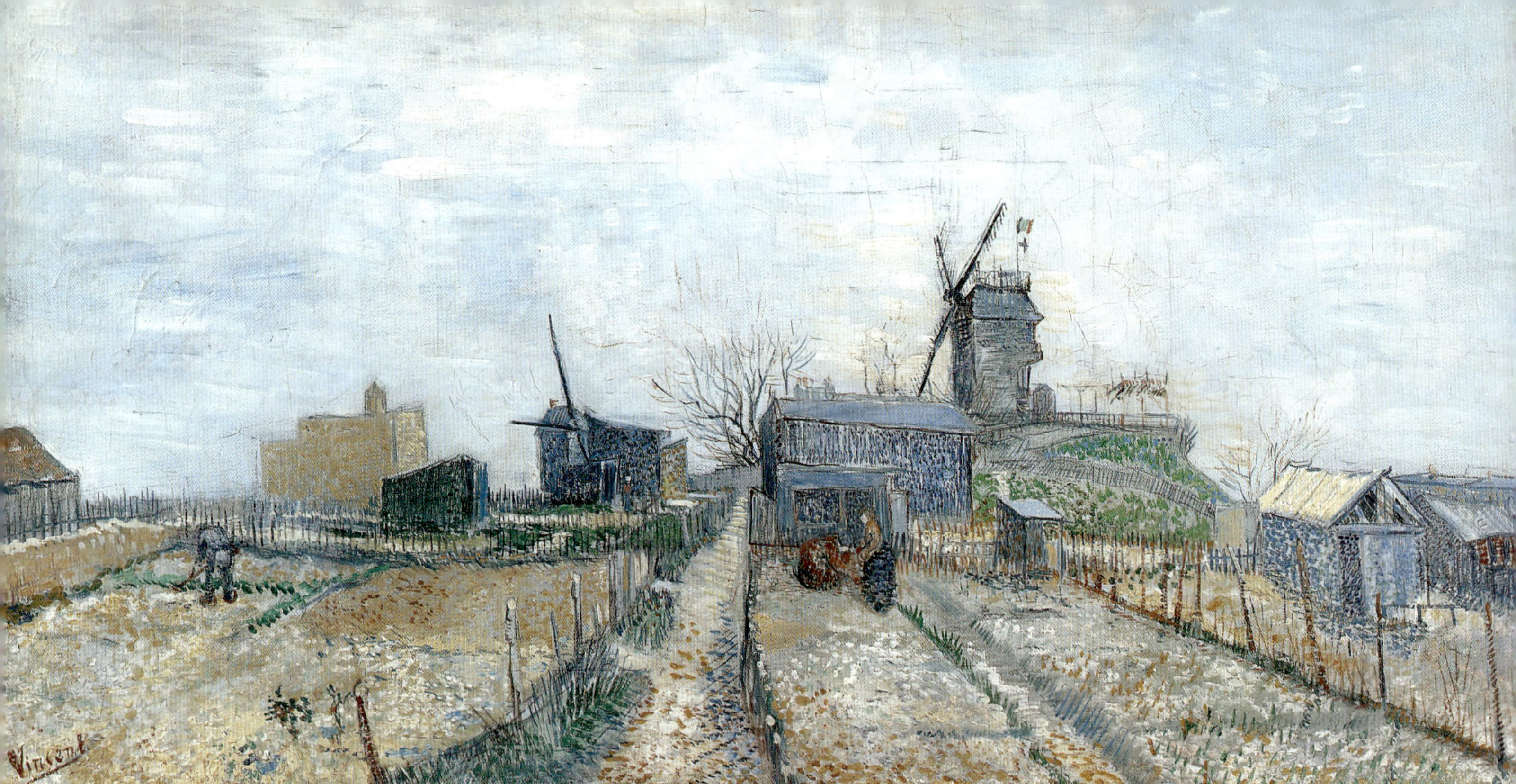

Vincent Willem van Gogh was born on March 30, 1853 in the village of Groot-Zundert in the province of Brabant in the Netherlands. The eldest surviving child of Theodorus van Gogh and Anna Cornelia Carbentus, he was named after their first son, who had been born on the same date one year earlier but died in infancy. Five more children followed Vincent: Anna Cornelia, Theodorus, Elisabetha, Willemina, known as Wil, and Cornelius Vincent.

Vincent's father, Theodorus van Gogh, was descended from a well-established bourgeois family. After studying theology, he became a Dutch Reformed pastor and an active practitioner of Christian Humanism. His wife Anna ran the modest household but was also an avid amateur botanist, recording her observations of flowering plants in accomplished watercolor sketches.

In addition to home instruction, Vincent attended the village school in Zundert for a year (1861) and was later sent to boarding schools in Zevenbergen (1864–1866) and Tilburg (1866–1868). A competent, but not distinguished, student, Vincent did possess a natural talent for languages and rapidly learned both French and English. He was an enthusiastic reader and from boyhood he enjoyed fiction as well as works on the natural sciences.

There was little in Vincent's youth to indicate any special inclination toward the arts. His earliest surviving drawings date to the time before he entered his first term at boarding school, but they appear to be copy work with little evidence of skill. The academy at Tilburg had a progressive drawing master named C. C. Huysman, who encouraged his students to study directly from nature as well as to make copies of masterworks. The extent to which he influenced Vincent cannot be judged, but even before his schooling young Vincent had been fascinated by first-hand observation of nature. From his early childhood, his parents had taken him

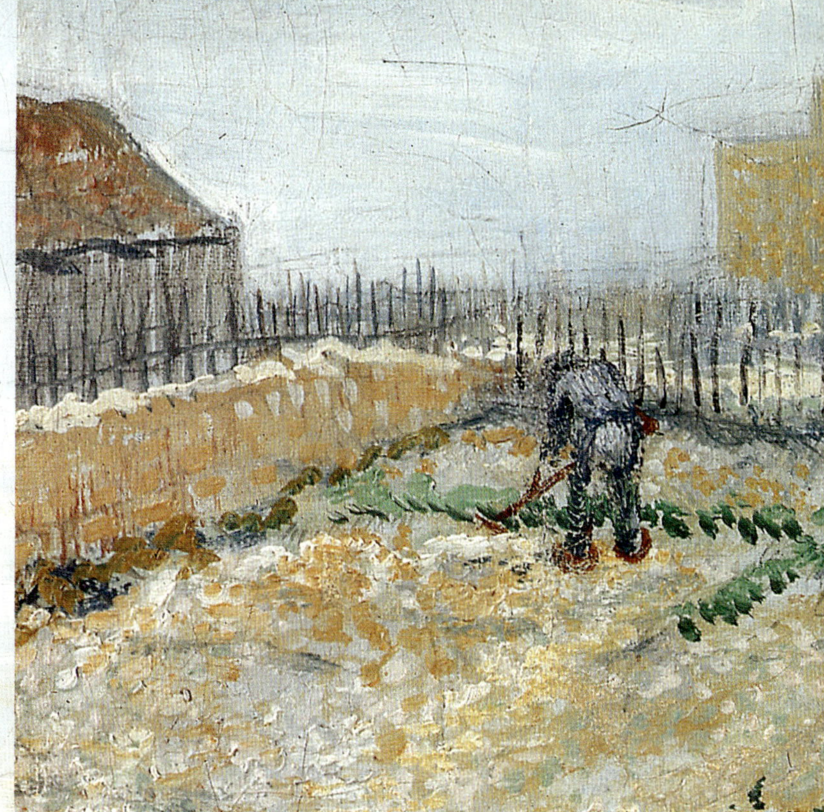

Vegetable Gardens and the Moulin de Blute-Fin on Montmartre
LEFT AND RIGHT
FEBRUARY–MARCH 1887. VAN GOGH MUSEUM, AMSTERDAM

Following the path pioneered by the Barbizon School and the Impressionists, Vincent believed in the integrity of *plein-air* painting. By working on the spot, he gained a sensitivity to the visual effects of light and color, seen in the nuances of tone in the sky and the flickering white touches on the fields in this painting. In the later years of the nineteenth century, the outskirts of the district of Montmartre were undeveloped and featured communal allotments, cottage gardens, and windmills. Emile Bernard attributed Vincent's urge to paint "the humble shanties of Montmartre where the lower middle classes come to cultivate their tiny pieces of sand in the early morning sun," to his reading of Emile Zola's naturalist novels, but whenever Vincent lived in the city he longed for the countryside.

on long walks through the woods where, perhaps following his mother's interest, he assembled collections of wild flowers, birds' nests, and insects.

Vincent left school at the age of sixteen to work and contribute to the family's finances. Through the influence of his Uncle Vincent, known as "Cent," he obtained a post as a junior clerk in a branch of art dealer and publisher Goupil et Cie in The Hague. Vincent proved to be both adept and enthusiastic in his work, and in June 1873, the company transferred him to their London establishment. Theo, his younger brother, followed him into the business, taking his position in The Hague. Always close, the brothers began a regular correspondence. In his letters Vincent confided his most private thoughts and he came to rely upon Theo's sympathy and support throughout his life.

New influences shaped Vincent's interest in England. While he admired a few English artists—including John Everett Millais and George Boughton—he also became fascinated with popular illustrated journals, particularly the *Illustrated London News* and the *Graphic*. He favored social realist images, depicting the struggle of the poor, which he clipped out and kept in a file for reference. His heightened sensitivity toward the less privileged was accompanied by an intensifying spirit of piety. Vincent's interest in the business of art waned in the wake of a mounting desire to give service to needy communities.

When Vincent failed to fulfill his initial promise in the business, the Goupil company transferred him from city to city, ultimately dismissing him in April 1876. A period of restlessness—fueled by his pious aspirations—followed. He served briefly as an assistant to a school master in England, but, seized with a passion to preach, he returned to Holland, seeking the support of his family in his new mission. Uncle Cent found him a position as a clerk in a

The Courtesan (after Kesaï Eisen) RIGHT
SEPTEMBER–OCTOBER 1887. VAN GOGH MUSEUM, AMSTERDAM

Cover of *Paris Illustré: Le Japon* FAR RIGHT
MAY 1886. VAN GOGH MUSEUM, AMSTERDAM

During the summer of 1887, Vincent made three copies in oil after Japanese prints. One was from the cover of a journal in Vincent's possession, featuring a reproduction of Kesaï Eisen's *The Courtesan* (1820s). For this work, he traced the figure, and overlaid the tracing with squares to transfer the image to his canvas. The result is a free interpretation rather than a strict translation. Although the pattern on the kimono follows the original, Vincent brightened the colors and loosened the rigid formality. He set his figure against a thickly impastoed background of gold, framed in a yellow border. The images behind her—blooming lily pads, feeding cranes, swaying bamboo, and a pair of frogs—were in part borrowed from other sources, including Toyokuni III's print *Geishas in a Landscape* and Yoshimaru's volume *A New Book of Incests*, but their combination in this decorative scheme was Vincent's own invention.

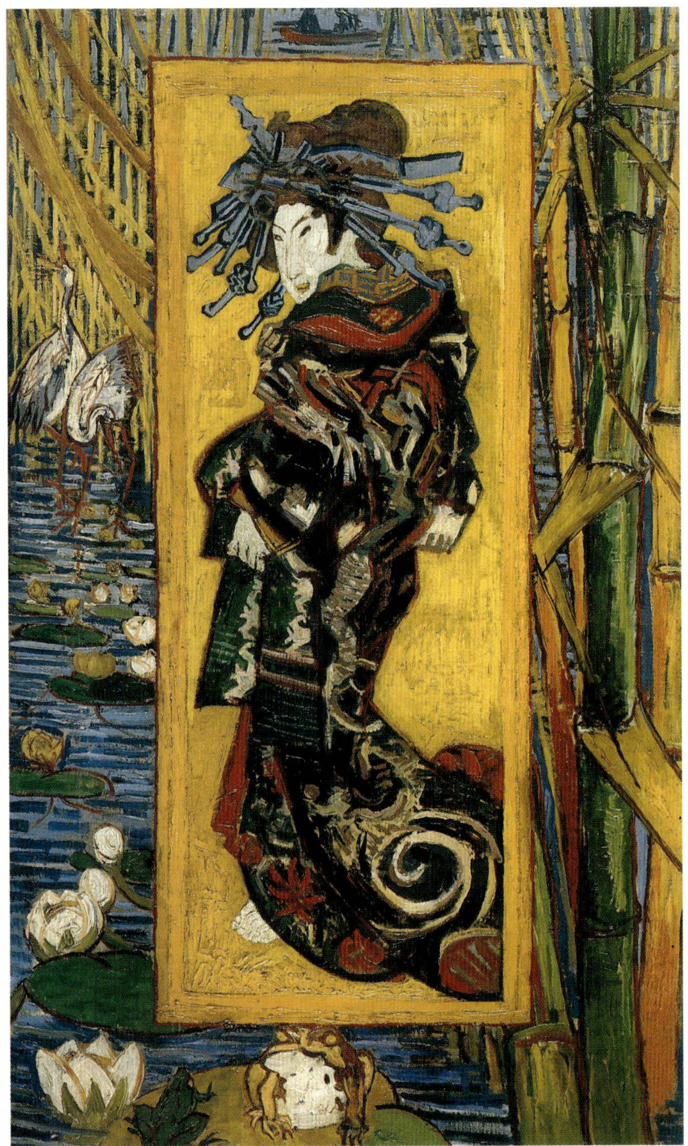

bookstore in Dordrecht, hoping that the salary would be put toward his education. But Vincent did not stay in the job, and in May 1877 he moved to Amsterdam to prepare for the qualifying examinations for a university course in theology. Once there, he neglected his studies, devoting his time instead to projects such as making a multilingual translation of the Bible and drawing meticulous maps of the Holy Land.

By July 1878, Vincent had abandoned his university plans. He began training for an evangelical ministry, but after the three-month probationary period he was denied an official post. Relying on his family's support, he moved to a community in the Borinage, a poor Belgian mining district beset with labor disputes, where he became a lay preacher. Vincent's now fanatical devotion led him to live a life of self-imposed sacrifice. Equating abstention with piety, he lived in a shack, ate only enough to stay alive, and

dressed in rags, having given away most of his possessions to the local poor. In July 1879 his superiors in the church intervened, and Vincent was prohibited from preaching. By the end of the year, the deeply religious tone of his letters to Theo had changed, revealing a different sense of mission: Vincent declared his desire to become an artist.

A new vocation

Vincent embraced his new vocation with the intensity of his recent religious calling. In letters to Theo and to his former employer Tersteeg, he asked for art materials, prints to copy, and Charles Bargue's drawing manual, *Exercises au fusain*. Theo, now promoted to the Paris office of Goupil et Cie, began to send his brother a monthly allowance; his generous support would continue throughout Vincent's life. Vincent's early subjects revealed his enduring sympathy with the downtrodden; beginning with drawings of the miners of the Borinage, he defined himself as an artist of working people and ordinary things.

Now a different kind of restlessness set in. Torn between a desire to work on his own and the recognition that formal study would improve his technique, Vincent moved back and forth from the city to the countryside. In October 1880, he enrolled in the academy in Brussels for classes in anatomical drawing and perspective. By April 1881, he tired of the regimen and left for an extended stay at his parents' home in Etten, where he drew landscapes, as well as figures. Over the summer, on Tersteeg's advice, he cultivated a relationship with Anton Mauve, his cousin by marriage and a member of The Hague School. In December, Vincent moved to The Hague, where Mauve gave him informal instruction in color theory.

During this period, Vincent suffered a physical decline. His poor nutrition caused stomach disorders and dental problems, and a stubborn case of gonorrhea required a three-week hospitalization. Relations with his parents became strained. They believed that their eldest son was chasing a capricious dream, and his behavior—refusing to join the family at Christmas, openly living with a prostitute and her children, and declaring his intention to marry her—struck them as deliberately defiant. Angry with his decisions, his parents also feared for his health and stability.

In the autumn of 1883, Vincent left The Hague, feeling that Mauve had no more to teach him and that family life and a career in the arts were irreconcilable. He traveled to Drenthe in northern Holland, again seeking inspiration among the rural workers. By December, plagued by intense loneliness, he joined his parents in Nuenen, where the previous year his father had been assigned to a parish post. Although emotionally estranged from his family, Vincent attended to his mother when she was bedridden with a broken leg in January 1884, and he was grief-stricken at the death of his father in March of the following year.

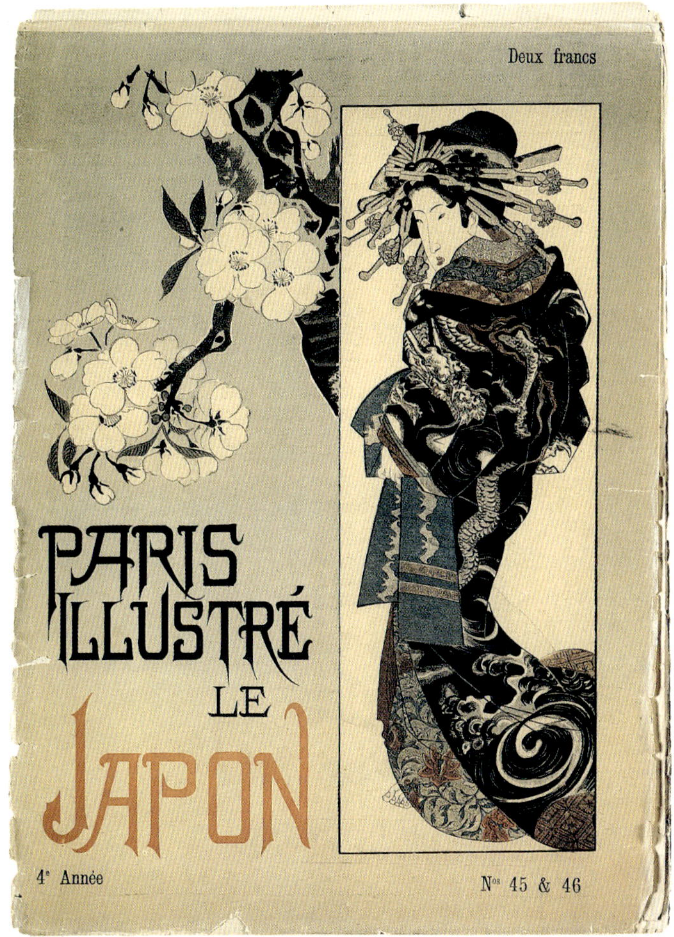

*"Since it is
winter, look
here, let me
go quietly on
with my work;
if it is that of
a madman,
well, so much
the worse, I
can't help it."*

LETTER TO THEO,
JANUARY 1889

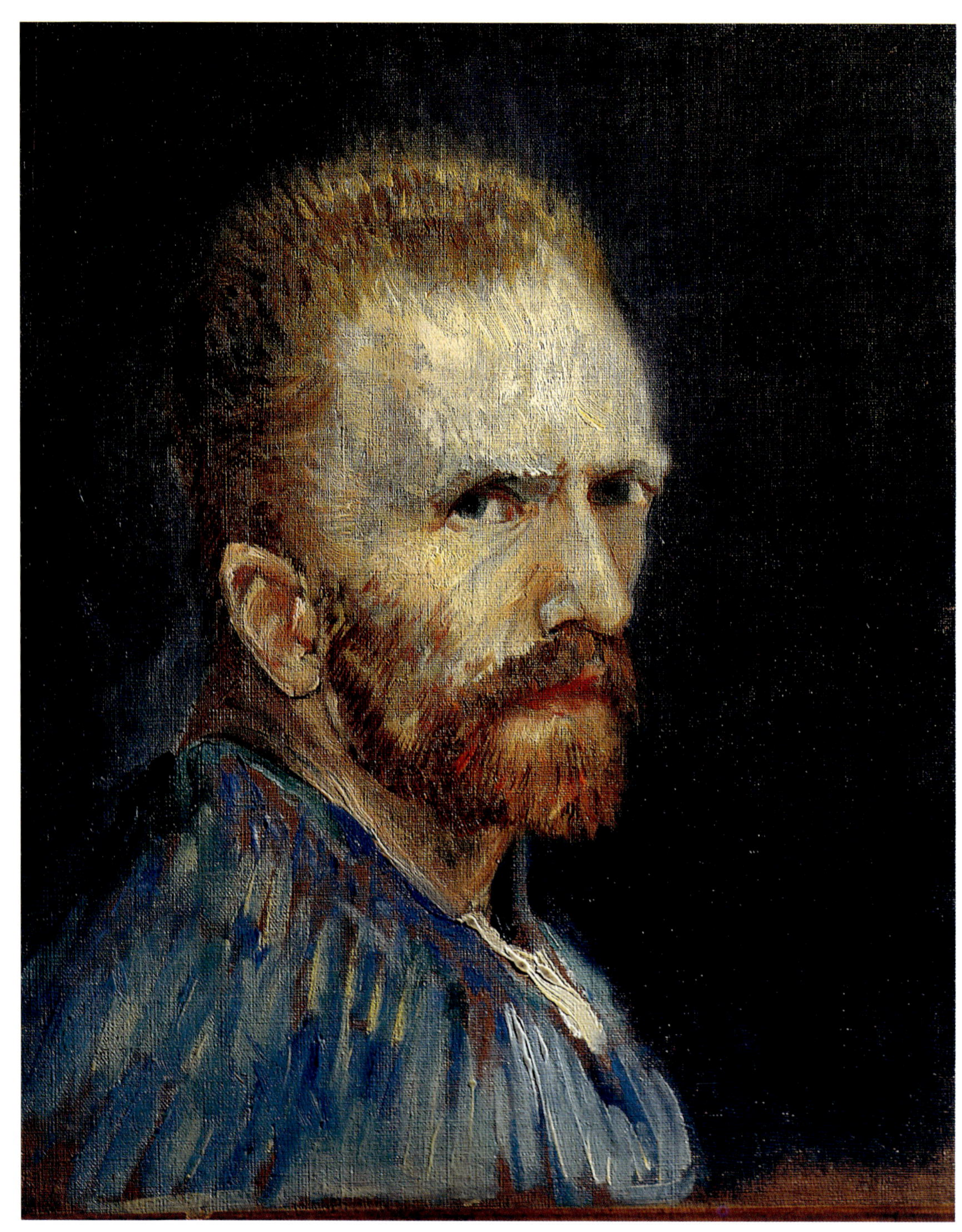

Vincent worked ceaselessly in Nuenen, drawing figures and portraits of the local farm workers. His first distinctive style emerged in *The Potato Eaters* (Van Gogh Museum, Amsterdam), painted in the spring of 1885. The somber palette, dominated by tones of brown, and the roughly drawn faces of the rugged peasants, expressed Vincent's desire to paint the spirit of the earth. But by autumn, he sought a change in his environment, moving briefly to Amsterdam, and then settling in Antwerp at the end of November. He enrolled in classes at the Ecole des Beaux-Arts early in the new year, but repeatedly expressed a need for a change of scenery in his letters to Theo. He proposed to visit Theo in June, after spending the spring in Nuenen. But, early in March, Theo received a note scrawled in black crayon from a railroad porter, imploring, "Do not be cross with me for having come all at once like this; I have thought about it so much, and I believe that in this way we shall save time. Shall be at the Louvre from midday on or sooner if you like" (Letter 459). Vincent had come to live with his brother in Paris.

An artistic community

Sharing his brother's apartment in Montmartre, Vincent was able to take part in the most advanced artistic community in Europe. Theo, now working for Boussod and Valadon (who had taken over the administration of Goupil et Cie), managed a gallery in Montmartre, featuring contemporary work. Through his brother, Vincent met many of the artists involved in the original Impressionist exhibition, including Monet, Degas, and Pissarro. That spring he attended the last Impressionist exhibition, where he saw Georges Seurat's experiment in optical divisionism, *Sunday Afternoon in the Isle of the Grand Jatte*. It excited him to share his ideas with the more daring painters of the day, including Paul Signac, Henri de Toulouse-Lautrec, and Paul Gauguin.

Self-Portrait, Summer
SUMMER 1887. WADSWORTH ATHENEUM, HARTFORD, CONNECTICUT

Vincent began his relentless and highly charged self-investigation through portraiture during his stay in Paris. Many explanations for his fascination with making self-portraits can be cited, one being that without ready funds to hire models, an artist like Vincent could always depict his own visage. But the intensity of his expression and the fixed gaze that demands the attention of the viewer suggest that Vincent used these portraits to explore his deepest emotions. This rich and brooding image was painted during his second summer in Paris. It demonstrates his new command of tone and brush stroke, pointing to the daring contrasts of color and the heavily applied paint that would characterize his mature style.

Vincent drew energy and inspiration from these new surroundings. He became a devoted *plein-air* painter, setting up his easel in the roads of Montmartre and in the suburb of Asnières with fellow painters Paul Signac and Emile Bernard. The claustrophobic quality of his dark Nuenen style disappeared. Most of all, he explored the use of color. Through the summer and well into the autumn he painted more than thirty bouquets, using his study of flowers to master the range of natural hues.

Like many of his contemporaries, Vincent was intrigued with Japanese prints. He began to collect them in Antwerp, writing to Theo that his studio room above a paint shop "is not too bad, especially as I have pinned up a number of Japanese prints on the walls which amuse me very much" (Letter 437). In Paris, during the summer of 1887, Vincent made three closely observed copies of individual prints—Hiroshige's *The Plum Tree Teahouse at Kameido* and *Sudden*

Shower on the Great Bridge, and Kesaï Eisen's *The Courtesan* —to gain first-hand knowledge of the aesthetic and to translate its qualities into his own technique. He came to associate everything pure, strong, and natural in art with Japanese prints; for Vincent, Japan was less a geographic location than an artistic ideal.

Vincent's years in Paris transformed his art and confirmed his own identity as an artist. But the stimulation of urban life and the sophisticated community drained him. He felt awkward in social situations, and he found few chances to display his paintings. Once again, Vincent neglected his health, and the brutal early winter of 1887 convinced him that he needed a change. He chose to go to Arles, believing

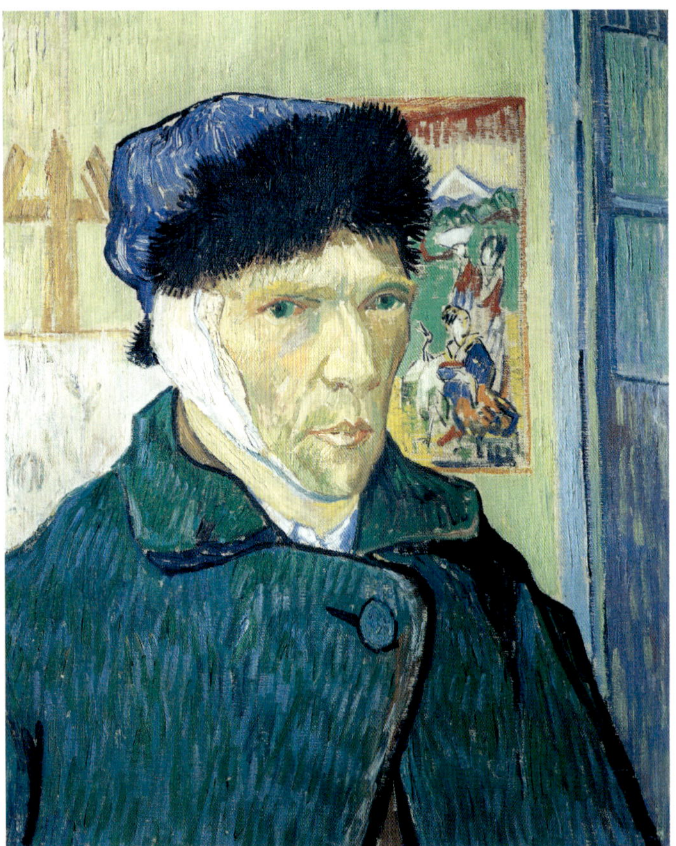

that the southern climate would improve his well-being and that the countryside would restore his equilibrium. On February 21, the day after he arrived in Arles, Vincent wrote to his brother that he had made the right decision: "It seems to me almost impossible to work in Paris unless one has some place of retreat where one can recuperate and get one's tranquility and poise back. Without that, one would get hopelessly stultified" (Letter 463).

The move to Arles

From the beginning, Vincent associated Arles with his personal vision of Japan. Although the harsh weather was a surprise—he had been seeking the sun and warmth of the south—he compared the snowy terrain to a winter scene in a Japanese print. As the seasons changed, Vincent allowed nature to suggest his subjects. In early spring he painted the blossoming trees, and with the onset of summer, he found inspiration in the fields of blooming flowers. Color became his foremost consideration; he observed the bold contrasts in nature and matched the blues and yellows of his palette to the bright fields of irises under the strengthening sun. In Arles, Vincent led a simple life of focused work, modeled on his notion of the life of Japanese craftsmen.

But Vincent longed for companionship, fellow artists to work with him in his "Studio of the South." He extended invitations to Emile Bernard and Paul Gauguin, and in anticipation, prepared one of the rooms he rented in the "Yellow House," a small building on the Place Lamartine in Arles. Through the late summer and early fall, he painted many sunflowers to decorate the white walls of the room; for Vincent, the large, bright blossom became a symbol of his dream of an artist's colony.

Sensitive to his brother's loneliness, Theo persuaded Gauguin to make the journey south to Arles. He arrived on October 23, and, at first, he appeared to provide ideal

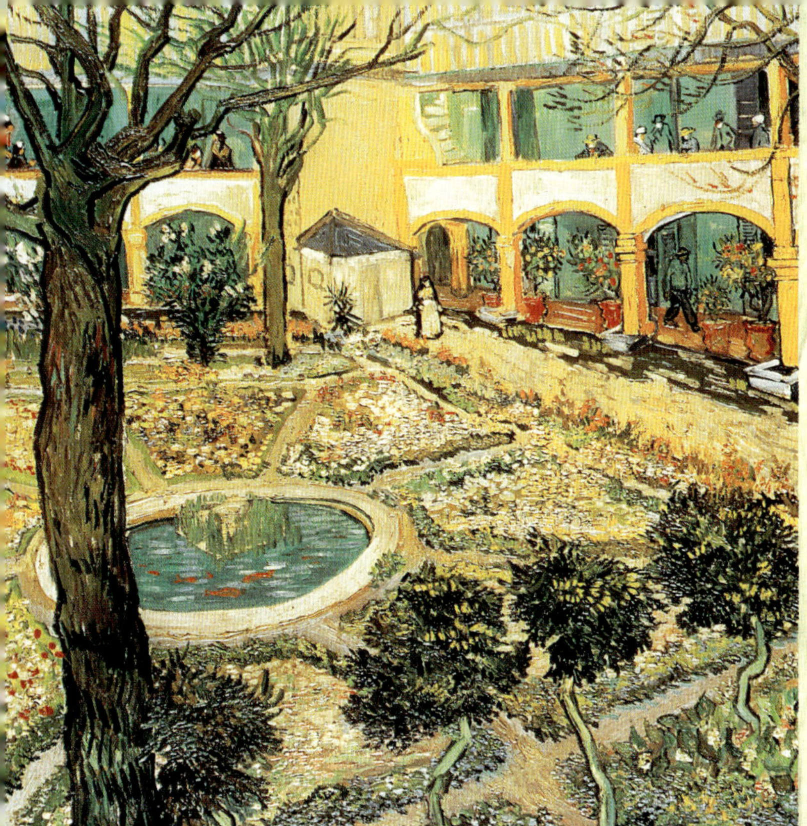

Self-Portrait with Bandaged Ear FAR LEFT
JANUARY 1889. COURTAULD INSTITUTE, LONDON

After the incident of his mutilation of his own ear, Vincent painted two self-portraits while he still wore heavy bandages. In this painting, he appears as a convalescent, wrapped in a thick wool coat, with his fur-trimmed hat pulled down over the dressings. Behind him is a Japanese print, Toyokuni III's *Geishas in a Landscape,* which had been in his collection at least since he lived in Paris. The print recalls the hopes he brought to Arles, but his weary posture and sorrowful gaze express the grim recognition that his life had irrevocably changed.

Courtyard in the Hospital at Arles LEFT AND BELOW
APRIL 1889. OSCAR REINHART COLLECTION, WINTERTHUR

While in hospital in Arles, Vincent made several drawings and paintings of the hospital garden. Here, he selected a high point of view, suggesting perhaps that he had set his easel on the balcony above the courtyard. The flowerbeds, radiating in wedge-shaped plots around the fountain in a traditional formal pattern, mark a contrast to the freer compositions he painted off the grounds.

company for Vincent. They worked together, shared their expenses, and Gauguin saw to it that Vincent ate more regularly, cooking him nourishing meals. But their close companionship began to stifle Gauguin and made Vincent feel anxious, and their lively debates about art soon heated into arguments. On December 23, according to Gauguin's account, Vincent confronted him with a razor. Gauguin claimed to have stared him down, and Vincent retreated to the Yellow House where he was found the next morning, bleeding profusely from a self-inflicted wound to his left ear. What drove him to this desperate state remains unclear, but his heightened emotions, exacerbated by his irregular eating habits and abuse of alcohol, may have triggered the first of the psycho-motor seizures that would continue to plague him for the rest of his days.

Vincent was taken to the hospital, where he was treated for blood loss and potential infection. Within a few weeks

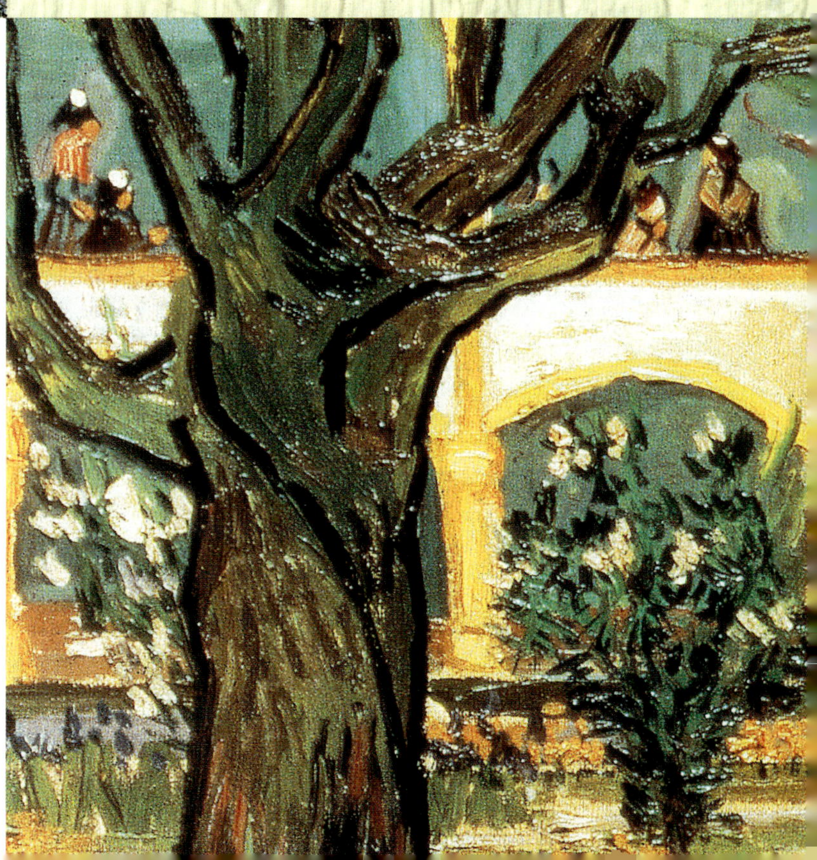

"For instead of trying to reproduce exactly what I see before me, I make more arbitrary use of color to express myself more forcefully."

LETTER TO THEO, AUGUST 1888

The Starry Night
JUNE 1889. THE MUSEUM OF MODERN ART, NEW YORK

Painted in June, just a month after Vincent voluntarily admitted himself to the asylum at Saint-Paul-de-Mausole, *The Starry Night* appears to reflect the turbulent turn of events that led to his self-imposed confinement. But from his first days in Provence, Vincent had expressed a wish to paint a "starry night with cypresses." His room in Saint-Paul-de-Mausole looked out on the eastern sky, presenting a vista to inspire him. Dominated in the foreground by a dark, twisting stand of trees, the panoramic terrain of *The Starry Night* seems to roll back into the distance under a chaotic sky. The stars, with their swirling auras of thick impasto, vibrate against the bright blue heavens. The orange-yellow of the crescent moon heightens the tonal contrast, recalling Vincent's sense of freedom in the "arbitrary use of color to express [himself] more forcefully."

he was released to convalesce alone—Gauguin had left Arles. Vincent attempted to dismiss his fear in his letters to Theo, describing his recent crisis as "an attack of artistic temperament," but further hospitalizations for his chronic insomnia and intermittent hallucinations followed.

When his neighbors petitioned the mayor of Arles to have him forcibly readmitted to hospital because of his erratic behavior, Vincent relinquished his vision of the Studio of the South. As Theo had recently married he could not consider intruding on him, but he longed for help and companionship. In May, he admitted himself to Saint-Paul-de-Mausole, a psychiatric hospital in nearby Saint-Rémy-de-Provence. At first, he was confined to the hospital gardens, but as his condition stabilized, he was allowed off the grounds to paint in the company of an attendant. The cypress groves and olive trees, as well as the surrounding fields, restored his sense of connection with nature through his art.

In this sympathetic environment, Vincent managed to regain some sense of strength and purpose. His condition was diagnosed as a form of epilepsy, and even under these controlled circumstances, he suffered from sporadic, but profound, seizures. As a result, Vincent was periodically debilitated, unable to work in the aftermath of an attack. In the intervals between these unpredictable incidents, he was calm and lucid, well aware of the scope of his condition. He wrote to Theo: "As far as I can judge I am not really mad. You will see that the canvases I've done in the meantime are untroubled and no worse than the others" (Letter 580).

Returning north

In October 1889, Camille Pissarro recommended to Theo that Vincent move to Auvers-sur-Oise, just north of Paris, where he could live under the care of Dr. Paul Gachet, a physician and amateur artist. Plans were delayed by a severe

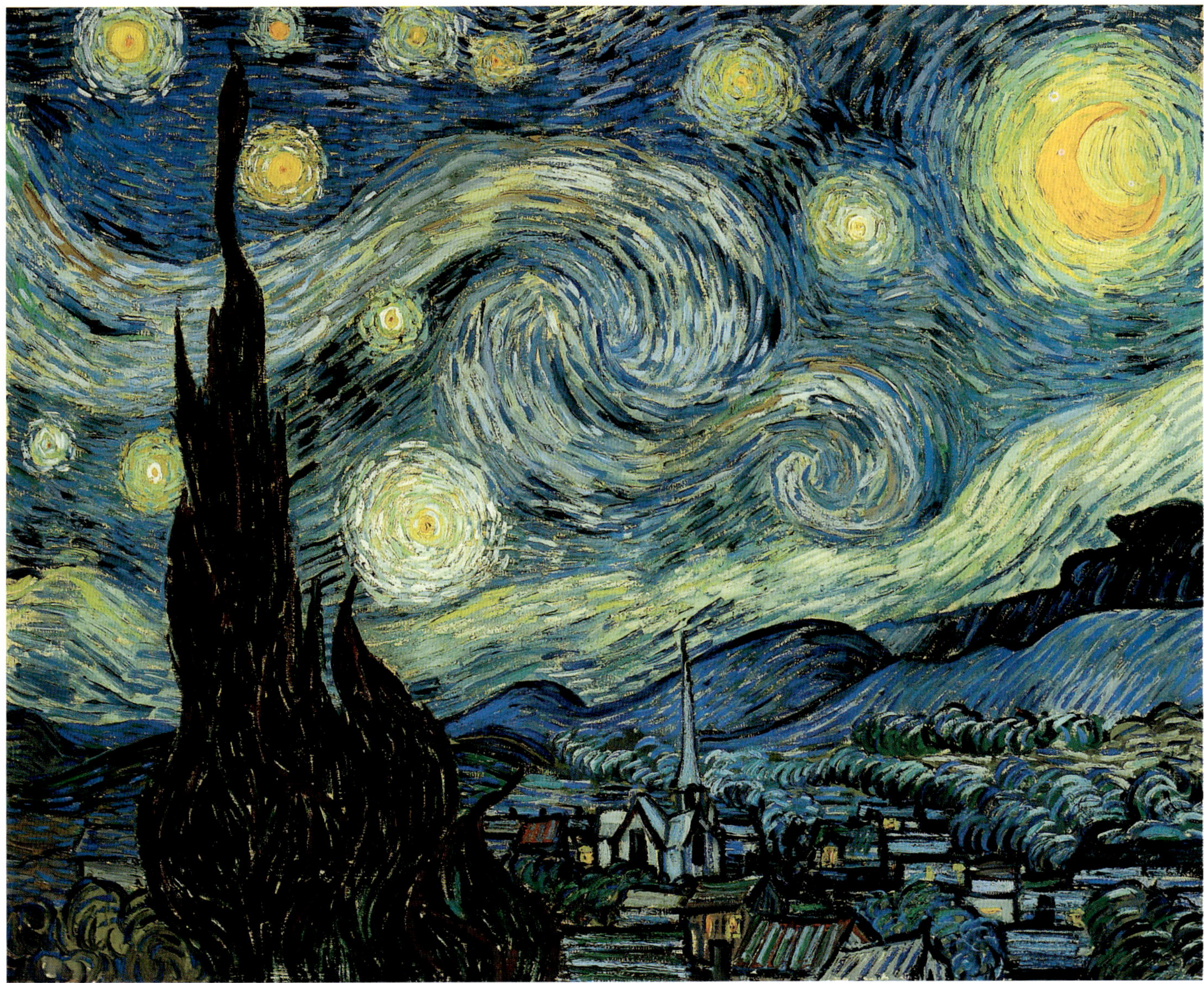

attack in December, and it was not until May 1890 that Vincent made the train journey to Auvers. He found his new circumstances comfortable and took an immediate liking to Paul Gachet, whom he described in a letter to his sister Willemina as being "a perfect friend" and almost "like another brother." Vincent sensed a deep empathy in Gachet: "So alike are we physically, mentally too. He is very nervous and most odd himself."

Vincent embraced his work with new conviction and a sense of tranquility, finding subjects that ranged from the garden at the house of Barbizon painter Charles Daubigny to the vast wheatfields that lay on the outskirts of Auvers.

But, on July 25, Theo received a letter from Vincent that he described in a note to his wife as "quite incomprehensible." Theo sadly wondered, "When will there come a happy time for him?" Two days later, Vincent shot himself in the stomach, while out in the wheatfields that had become the focus of his art. He died on July 29.

The funeral was held in Auvers, with Theo and a few friends in attendance. In a letter to Albert Aurier, the first critic to recognize the power of Vincent's painting, Emile Bernard described Vincent's coffin, covered with a simple white drape and "masses of flowers, the sunflowers that he so loved, yellow dahlias, yellow flowers everywhere. It was his favorite color, if you remember, symbol of the light that he dreamed of finding in the heart of his artworks."

The story of Vincent van Gogh's turbulent life has been told repeatedly in the century since his death. He, too, left many accounts of his experience: his self-portraits provide an intimate and unflinching view of his troubled inner existence, while his long, heartfelt correspondence with his brother lends insight to the issues on his mind. But another vision of Vincent can be observed in the paintings of fields and flowers that occupied him during the last, and most productive, years of his life. As he painted the bouquets and the flowering trees, the iris and the sunflower, and the vast fields, Vincent celebrated the deep connection of his art with nature. Within that bond, he found a brief and tranquil refuge, and at least for a time, a reason to work and live, feeling joy in his own existence.

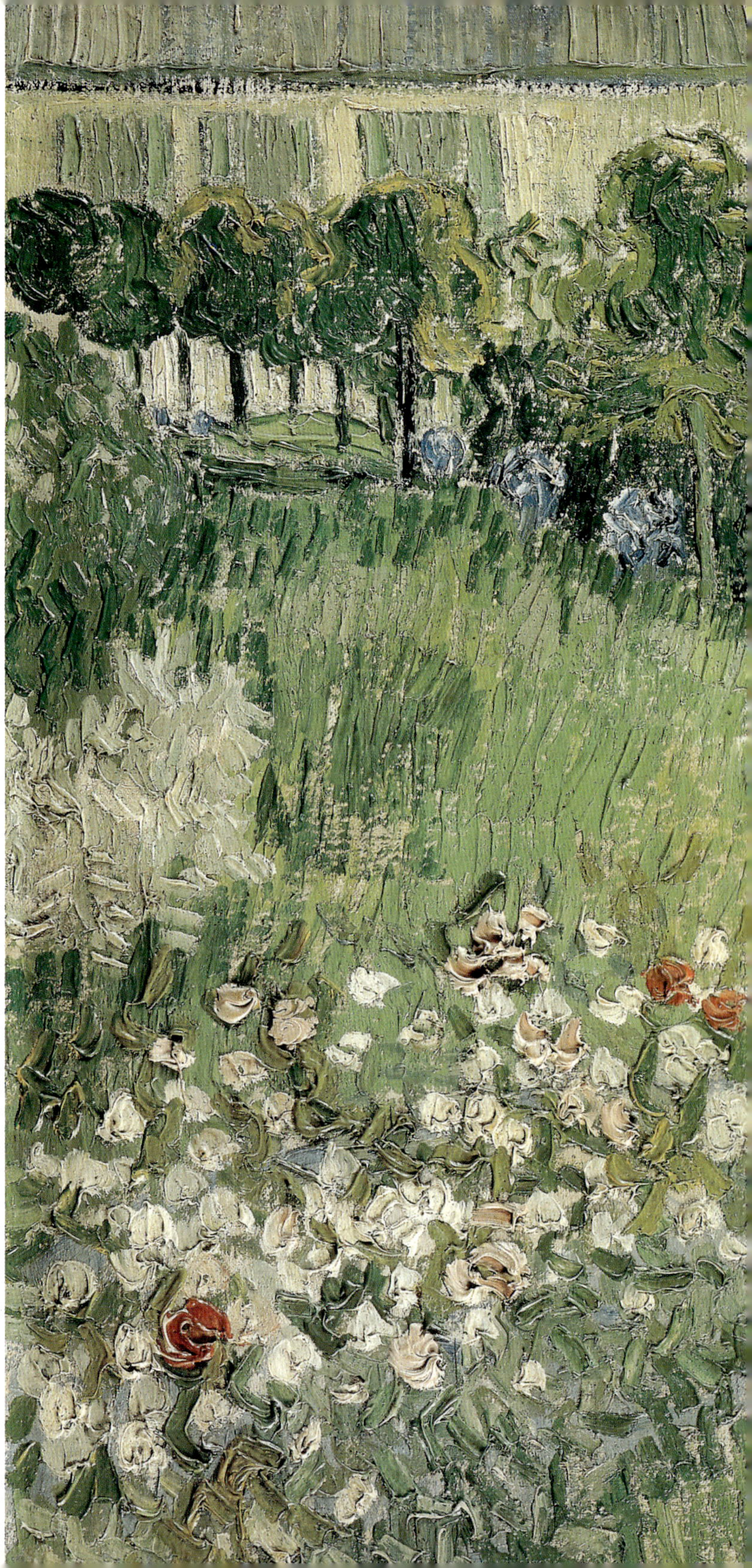

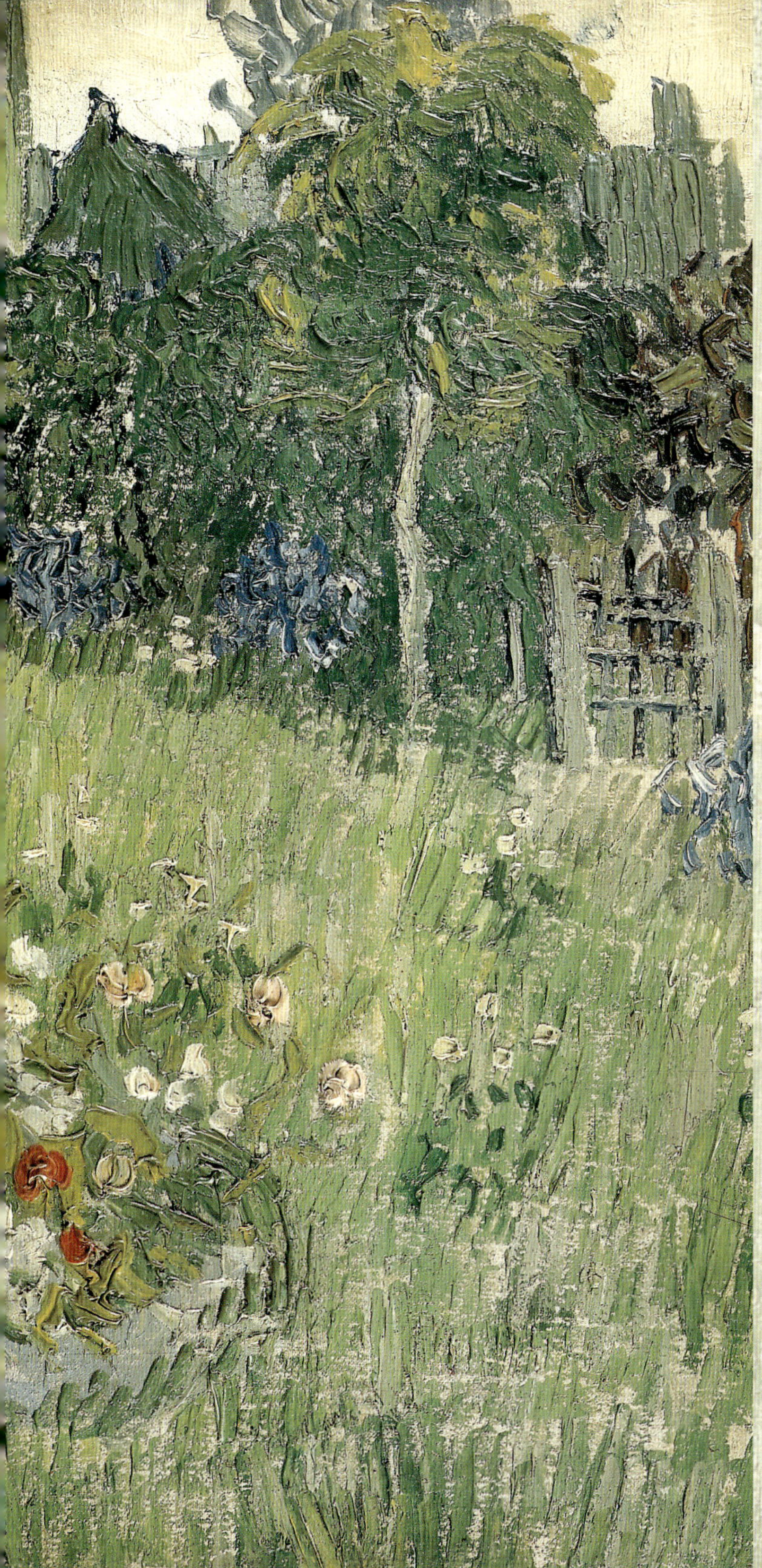

"But for one's health, as you say, it is very necessary to work in the garden and see the flowers growing."

Letter to his mother and Wil, Summer 1890

Daubigny's Garden
June 1890. Van Gogh Museum, Amsterdam

Charles-François Daubigny, a painter associated with the Barbizon School, was an early advocate of *plein-air* painting. When Vincent settled in Auvers, he was delighted to find that although the painter had died nineteen years earlier, Daubigny's widow still lived in his house. Vincent painted this portrait of Daubigny's garden and sent a sketch of the work to Theo, calling it "one of my most carefully thought-out canvases." The quiet palette, with its delicate tones of pink, green, and violet, shows a greater fidelity to what the eye sees in nature than his recent works, perhaps in tribute to the naturalist painter. And the light brush strokes, with touches of gleaming white highlights, recall the shimmering surfaces of Vincent's work in Paris, when he first discovered Impressionism.

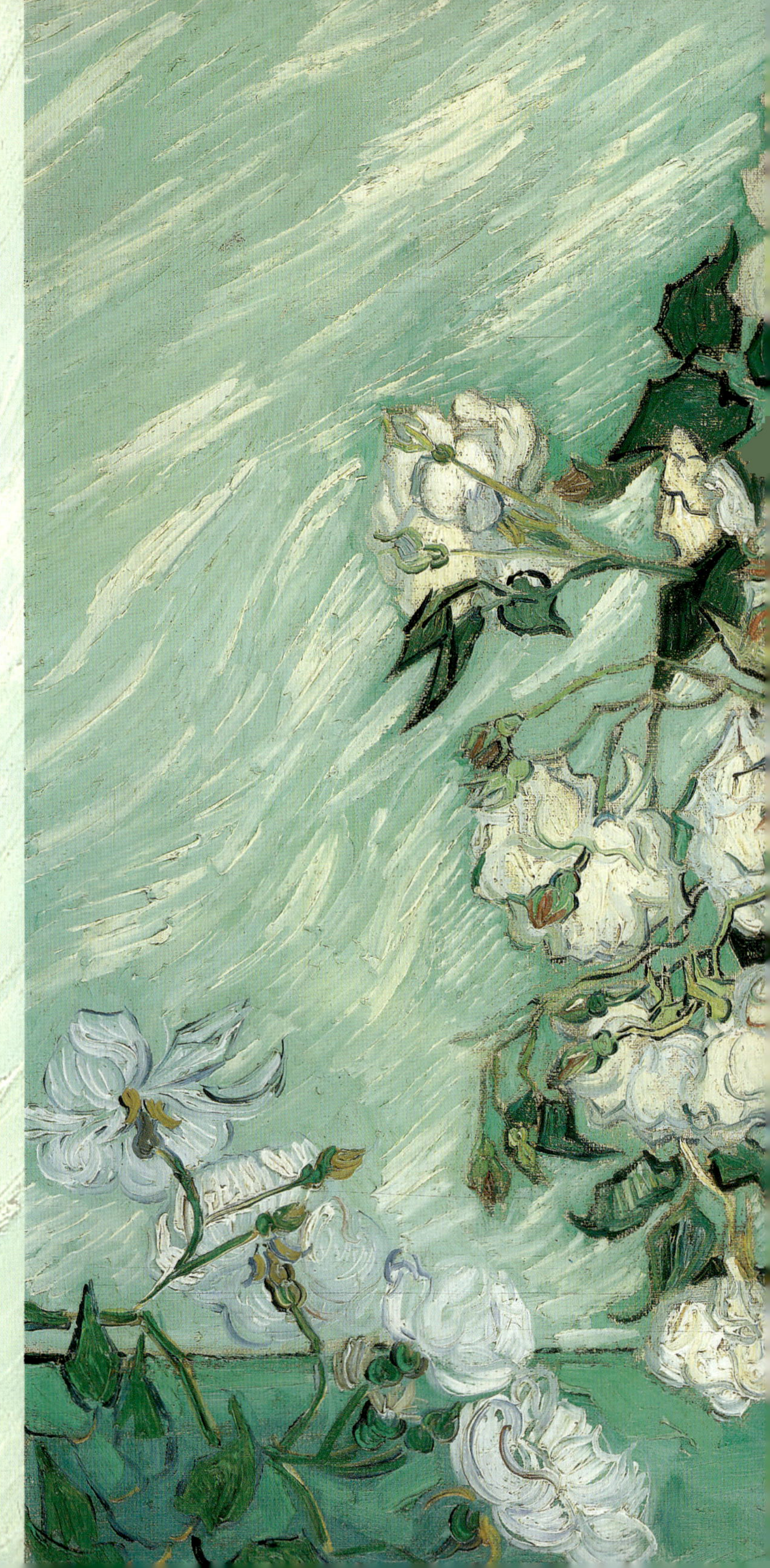

2
BOUQUETS

*"I painted hardly
anything but flowers
in order to get
accustomed to using
a scale of colors
other than gray."*

Letter to Theo, Autumn 1887

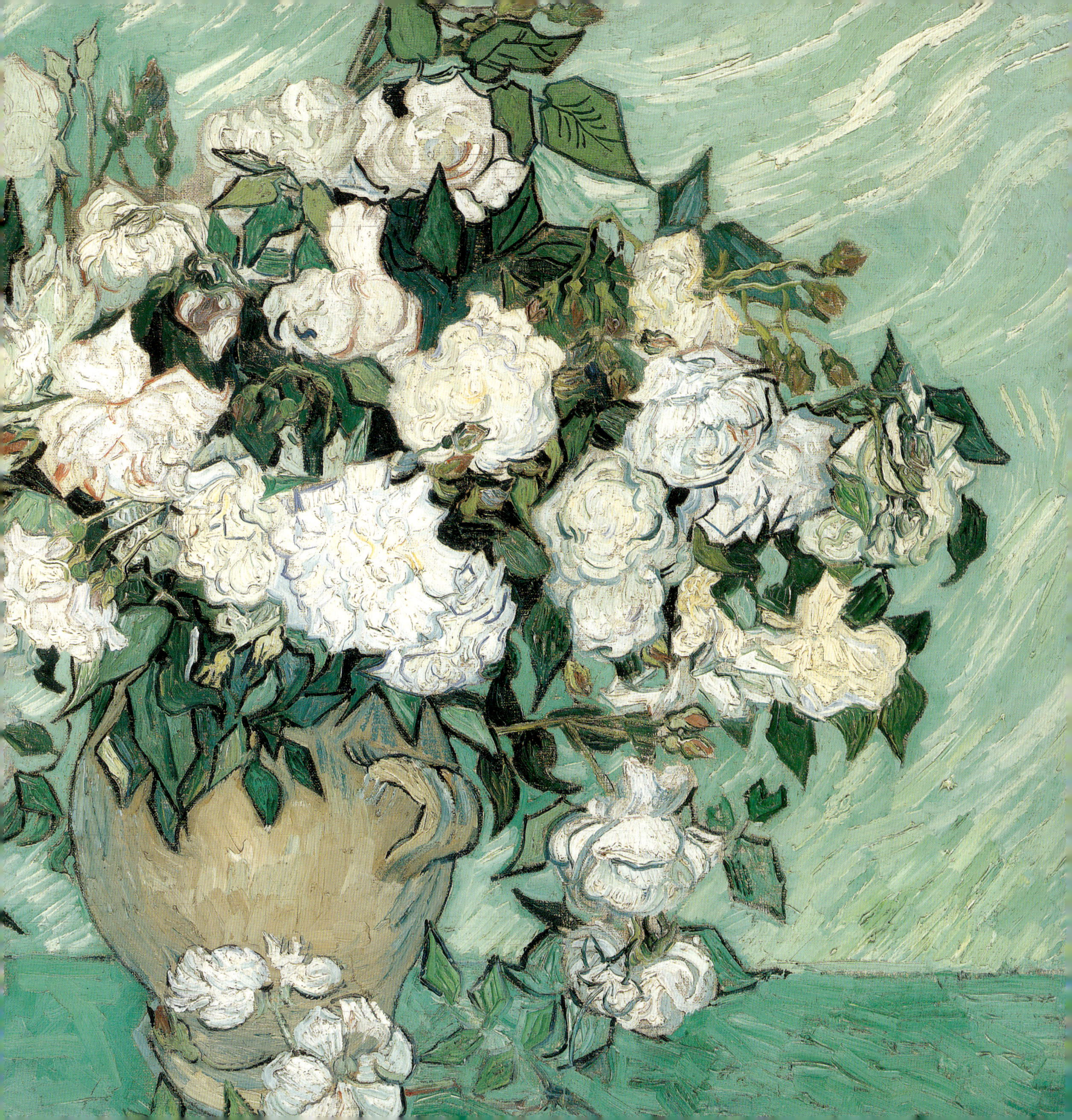

Poppies RIGHT
SUMMER 1886. WADSWORTH ATHENEUM, HARTFORD,
CONNECTICUT

The importance Vincent placed on his bouquets is revealed in a
letter to his friend Horace Livens, in which he announced he was
making great progress in his own art by concentrating on painting
flowers. In listing his various subjects, Vincent mentioned "red
poppies." *Poppies* dates from approximately the same time; in its bold
pairing of red and green, it illustrates Vincent's fascination with the
contrasting of a primary color with its complement. The touches of
pink in the unopened buds, the muted sienna on the table top, and
the sweeping dashes of blue in the background do little to temper
the visual vibrancy Vincent achieved with red and green.

Roses PRECEDING PAGES
MAY 1890. NATIONAL GALLERY OF ART, WASHINGTON, D.C.

Although the series of bouquets is distinctive to Vincent's Paris
period, he never lost interest in the subject. In subsequent years he
often painted bunches of flowers, favoring irises and sunflowers for
their vivid colors and their personal significance. Near the end of
his stay at Saint-Rémy, he painted several varied bouquets, reflecting
his enthusiastic anticipation of his move to Auvers. Writing to his
sister Wil he confided, "The last days in Saint-Rémy I worked like
a madman. Great bouquets of flowers, violet-colored irises, great
bouquets of roses." *Roses* is one of four large flower paintings Vincent
completed before his departure from the asylum. The masterful range
of color and the assured, articulated brush strokes reflect his newly
revived optimism. They also reveal the knowledge he gained in his
extended familiarity with the seemingly simple subject of bouquets.

Late in the summer of 1887, Vincent wrote to his sister Wil
from Paris. His letter was prompted by a written description
of plants in the rain that she had sent to him as evidence of
her aspirations toward a writing career. Vincent's response
was affectionate, filled with brotherly advice. He cautioned
her not to idealize the natural world, noting that "in nature
many flowers are trampled underfoot." But he also warned
her not to immerse herself too deeply in study; by doing
so she would neglect life's simple pleasures. He was frank
about his own mistakes, citing himself as someone "who
can count so many years of my life during which I lost any
inclination to laugh." He urged her to follow the path of
Voltaire's Candide, who learned to find joy and meaning
in life through the cultivation of his own garden.

Vincent felt his own experience in Paris bore sound
witness to the value of this advice. He had arrived there
with a single goal in mind: to work on his art. Regarding
his time in Nuenen and Antwerp as a preparatory stage—
akin to tilling the soil before planting—he was now able to
bring into blossom the form and color lying dormant in his
early efforts. He described how he had transformed his work
in his letter to Wil: "Last year I painted almost nothing but
flowers so as to get used to colors other than gray—pink,
soft or bright green, light blue, violet, yellow, glorious red."

The scope of his work in Paris was, in fact, much wider
than Vincent admitted. In this period of great exhilaration
and experimentation, he painted figure studies, landscapes,
and portraits as well as still lifes. And he infused new energy
into his technique by working out of doors, recording his
immediate impressions of light and atmosphere. During the
two years he lived and worked in Paris, Vincent painted
more than 230 pictures. Of these, thirty or more were floral
still lifes. As revealed to Wil, Vincent held these bouquets in
special regard. By painting flowers he had learned to work
with and appreciate the colors of nature.

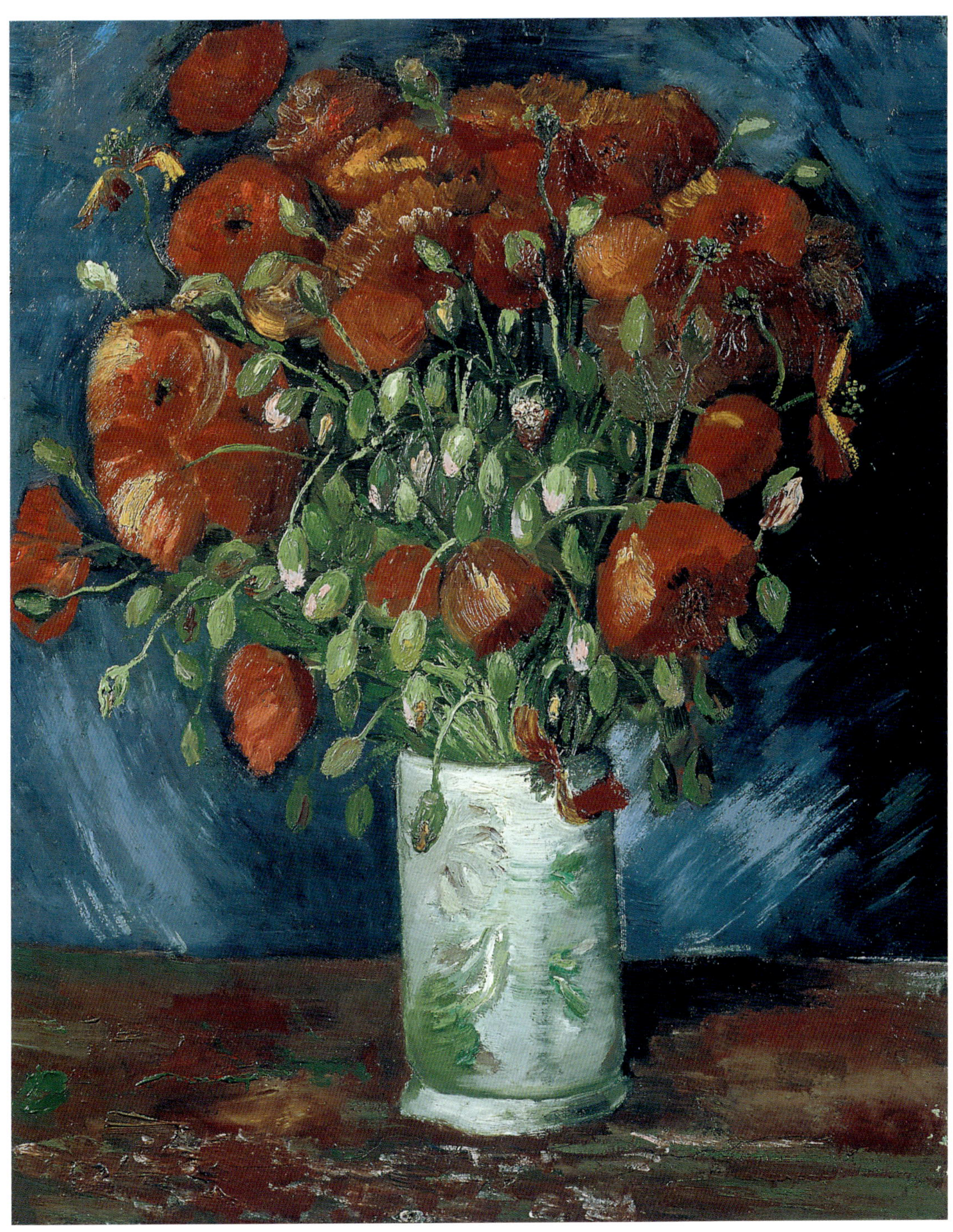

*"It is good to
love flowers...
they have been
with us from
the very
beginning."*

LETTER TO THEO,
MARCH 1877

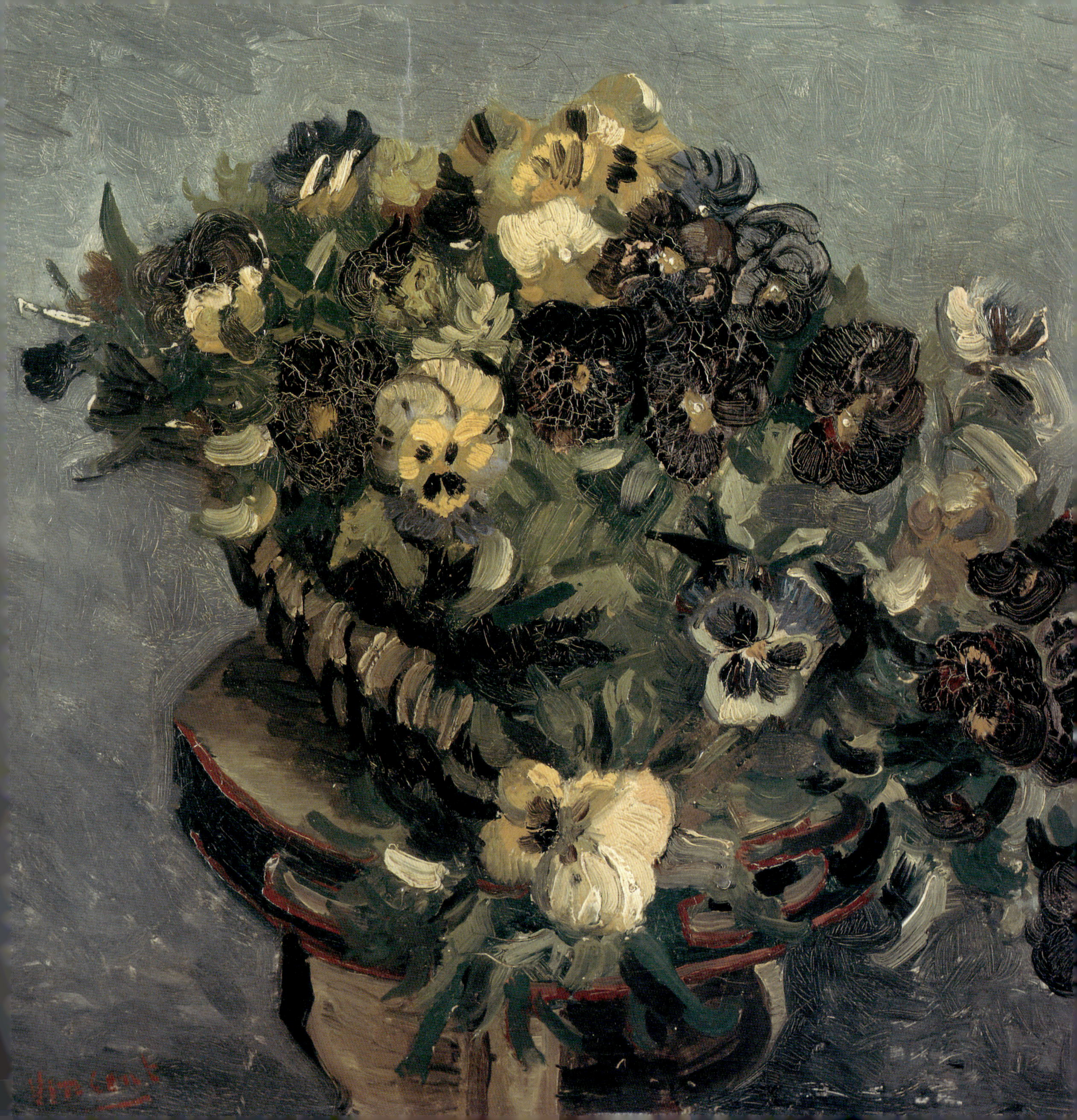

> *"You will see that
> by making a habit of
> looking at Japanese
> pictures you will love
> to make up bouquets
> and to do things with
> flowers all the more."*
>
> LETTER TO WIL, SEPTEMBER 1888

The "color question"

In the years before he moved to Paris, Vincent had made several attempts to "study the color question." The first came under the brief, informal tutelage of Anton Mauve. Related to Vincent through marriage into his mother's family, Mauve was one of the foremost figures in a Dutch school of painters based in The Hague.

Prompted by his former Goupil supervisor Tersteeg, Vincent visited Mauve in the summer of 1881 and asked him to review his drawings. Mauve presented him with a box of watercolors and suggested that he use them to add color to his work. In December, Vincent settled in The Hague, where he remained for more than a year, working to develop his technical skills. Mauve played a sporadic but important role in that development, urging Vincent to moderate the different tones in his painting and to follow the example of the painters of the Barbizon School in their

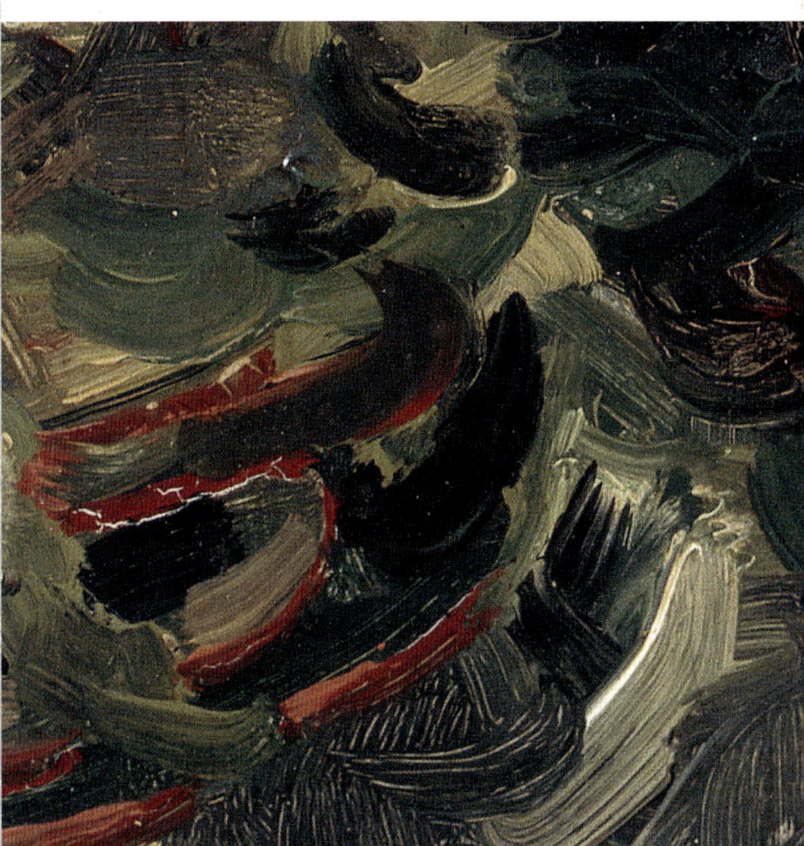

Bowl with Pansies LEFT AND RIGHT
SPRING 1886. VAN GOGH MUSEUM, AMSTERDAM

Primary and complementary colors in nature inspired Vincent's color theories. He believed that the contrast of complementaries gave a vital force to his painting. In this bouquet of pansies, the yellow and purple hues of the flowers dominate, while the green-flecked background and the red details of the tambourine provide a secondary harmony. Although traditionally pansies signal a poignant message— "you occupy my thoughts"—Vincent saw them as examples of a natural theory of color rather than a sentimental emblem. He acknowledged the seasonal cycle in his selection of flowers, painting pansies in the spring.

close but subtle rendering of natural effects. By the summer
of 1882, Vincent had begun to paint in oil.

His continued fascination with color is also borne out in
the detailed descriptions in his letters of the challenge of
rendering the shades of color in nature. Writing to Theo
of a woodland scene, he admitted, "it was hard to paint." He
explained that the ground cover needed to be dark, but
within the darkness was an astonishing array of hues: "more
red, yellow, brown ocher, black, sienna, wine-red, and even
a pale blond ruddiness. Then there is still the moss on the
ground, and a border of fresh grass, which catches light and
sparkles brightly, and is very difficult to get" (Letter 228).
Later in the same letter, he asked his brother if it would be
possible to purchase his paints wholesale, claiming that to
capture nature, "one must sometimes not spare the tube."

During the restless years that followed his stay in The
Hague, Vincent continued to study color. By reading the
published letters of Eugène Delacroix, Vincent expanded
his working knowledge of color theory and, like Delacroix,
used his observations of nature to illustrate and confirm
his beliefs. Writing to Theo from Nuenen, he described an
inherent system of color that he learned from watching the
seasons change: "Spring is tender, green young corn and
pink apple blossoms. Autumn is the contrast of the yellow
leaves with violet tones. Winter is the snow with black
silhouettes. But now, if summer is the contrast of blues
with an element of orange in the golden bronze of the
corn, one could paint a picture which expressed the mood
of the seasons in each of the contrasts of complementary
colors" (Letter 372).

Vincent's move to Antwerp late in 1885 brought more
discoveries. After working in the limited earth-brown color
range he created for *The Potato Eaters*, the robust, vital work
of Flemish master Peter Paul Rubens was a revelation.
Vincent characterized Rubens's style as bold and simple,

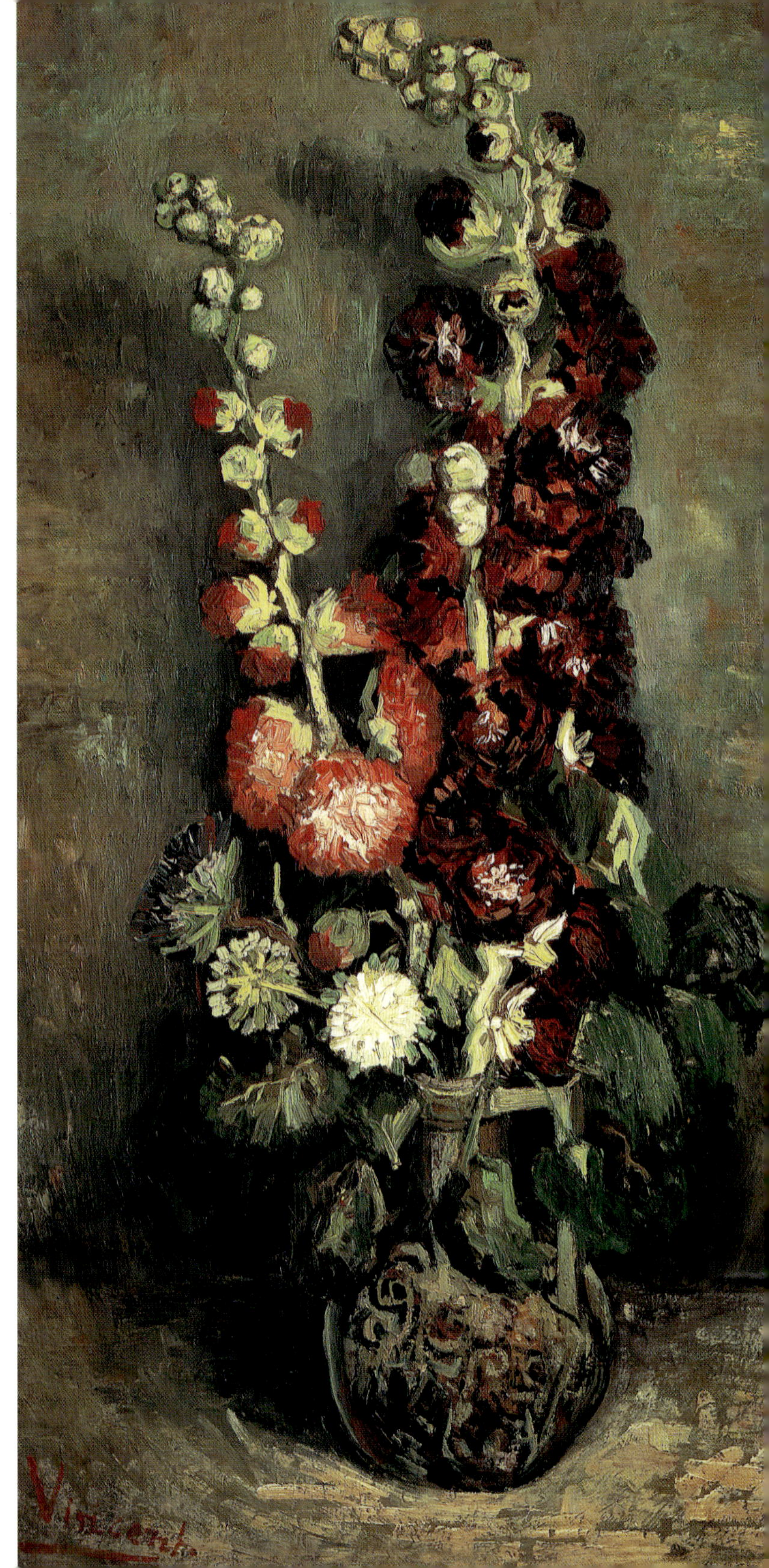

expressed through the vigor of his bright, red-based tones and thick, painterly brushwork. Studying Rubens's work first-hand also served to increase his understanding of Delacroix's ideas on color, for Delacroix readily admitted his own debt to Rubens. Vincent wrote to Theo: "What I admire so much in Delacroix, too, is that he makes us feel the life of things, and the expression, and the movement, that he *absolutely dominates his colors*." (Letter 439). But Vincent was also constructing color theories of his own, allying art with human experience. In a letter to Theo he made an essential observation: "What color is in a picture, enthusiasm is in life—it is no little thing to try to keep that enthusiasm" (Letter 443).

New experiences

Paris offered Vincent countless opportunities to extend his knowledge of the theoretical and practical application of color. Within a few weeks of his arrival, Vincent enrolled in the atelier of Fernand Cormon, a painter known for his epic scenes of prehistory. The length of Vincent's stay in the studio is uncertain—he may have attended classes there as late as November 1886—and the influence of Cormon's teaching on Vincent's emerging style was negligible. But in the atelier, known for its open-minded acceptance of new ideas, Vincent met young artists, such as Emile Bernard, Henri de Toulouse-Lautrec, and Louis Anquetin, who all shared his desire to discover fresh solutions to the traditional challenges of painting.

Vincent became an enthusiastic observer of the latest trends in contemporary art. Although long aware of the notoriety of the Impressionist exhibitions, his time in Paris gave him his first opportunity to study Impressionist works closely, to see precisely how the idea of a spontaneous visual response to a subject was expressed in color contrasts and broken brush strokes. He was intrigued by the new

Hollyhocks
JULY–SEPTEMBER 1886. KUNSTHAUS, ZURICH

Hollyhocks are a late summer flower, traditionally associated with motherhood and fecundity, but Vincent's decision to paint them reflects his interest in the seasons rather than the symbolic language of flowers. Worked in shades of red and green, *Hollyhocks* illustrates Vincent's belief that he could reflect the mood of the seasons in his colors. Concentrating on the analysis of tone, Vincent flattened the spatial planes of his composition; only a slight deepening of the background green into murky shadows marks the difference between the wall and the table top. The earthenware jug, with its squared handle and swirling decorative pattern, is the same as that used in the painting *Vase with Autumn Asters* (page 36–37).

scientific direction taken by artists such as Georges Seurat and Paul Signac. Their readings of optical theory led to the development of a technique known as divisionism, in which dots of pure color were dabbed side by side on the canvas, allowing the viewer's eye—rather than the painter's brush—to do the mixing. Eager for understanding, Vincent explored every new technique in his art, painting out of doors, lightening his palette, shortening his brush strokes, and even dabbing his canvas with contrasting dots of paint. But he conducted his most intense investigations into the use of color on his own, painting bouquets in his studio.

In his decision to paint bouquets, Vincent established his connection with a long tradition in Netherlandish painting. Flower painting was one of the many ways the "Little Masters" of the seventeenth century, such as Willem Kalf, Pieter Claesz, and Jacob van Walscappelle, demonstrated their astonishing ability to recreate in paint what the eye saw in nature. Vincent may have also chosen his subject out of admiration for the floral still lifes of Delacroix and Henri Fantin-Latour, whose work displayed passion and appealed to the senses with its dramatic contrasts of color. Flowers were a natural subject for the impressionist aesthetic—his contemporaries in Paris, painters such as Claude Monet, Pierre-Auguste Renoir, and Armand Guillaumin, all painted many flower pieces.

Vincent's choice also had mundane aspects—flowers made readily available models for little money. He could purchase an impressive variety of blooms and greenery daily from the flower market and arrange them as he liked in found containers, making an almost infinite range of contrast in color and texture. Often, the flowers were gifts from friends, as Theo explained in a letter to their mother: "He has acquaintances who send him a fine bunch of flowers to paint every week." With both limited means and

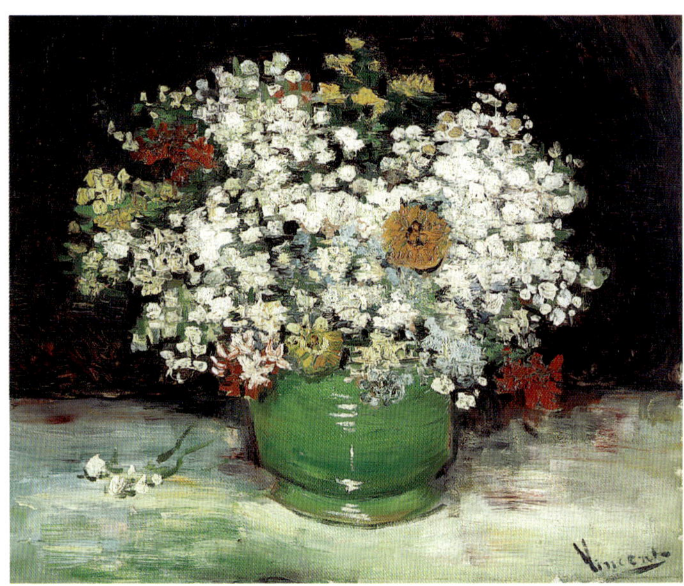

working space, flower painting was practical. But Vincent regarded his flower painting as an essential stage in his artistic development rather than an end in itself. His most compelling reason for painting bouquets of flowers was to master natural color.

In traditional still-life painting, each object had its own encoded meaning and the flower paintings by seventeenth-century Netherlandish masters followed this practice of loaded imagery. Individual flowers held conventional—and readily recognizable—messages, and the practice of reading flowers as emblems had a venerable heritage, dating back to the writings of classical Greece and Ancient Rome.

With his strong interest in the arts, Vincent would have been well aware of the lexicon of flower iconography. In fact, in Vincent's day, flower symbolism was being widely revived as "florigraphy," part of a thriving floral culture in Europe that had been on the rise since the early years of the nineteenth century. New publications addressed every aspect of botany—from science to sentiment—and among these were guides that assigned specific meanings to

Still-life: flowers (II) ABOVE RIGHT
SUMMER 1886. NATIONAL GALLERY OF CANADA, OTTAWA

With its limited palette of white and green, set against a moody background and punctuated only with red, orange, and gold, *Still-life: flowers* is reminiscent of the subtle floral paintings of Henri Fantin-Latour. But, when describing his series of bouquets, Vincent acknowledged a debt to only one artist—Adolphe Monticelli, who worked in Provence. Vincent admired Monticelli's floral still lifes for their vitality and richness. Their thick impasto inspired Vincent to use his paint freely, building up texture in heavy relief.

Flowers in a Glass Vase, **Jacob van Walscappelle** RIGHT
C. 1670. NATIONAL GALLERY, LONDON

Keen observation and consummate craftsmanship distinguish the tradition of still-life painting in seventeenth-century Netherlands. Jacob van Walscappelle (1644–1727) measured his skill by the accuracy of his rendering but also showed the sensual aspect of the visible world. He demonstrates the range of his technique in depicting a variety of textures from soft rose petals and the delicate skin of a strawberry to the smooth surface of the glass vase.

traditional blossoms, meanings that became known as the language of flowers. One of the new books devoted to floral symbolism was *Le Langage des Fleurs* by Charlotte Latour, which was published in France in 1819. Within a generation, counterparts to Latour's book appeared in Britain, Germany, and America, and the language of flowers became so popular that florigraphy lists were generally included in popular publications, such as etiquette books, almanacs, and household manuals. Although most of the florigraphy guides were written for women, the meanings they assigned became a standard feature of symbolic language and imagery in the later nineteenth century.

It is tempting, therefore, to search for coded meanings in Vincent's bouquets: reading anemones as abandonment, hollyhocks as fecundity, daisies as innocence, and poppies as consolation. But nothing in Vincent's correspondence suggests that he read the popular guides to the language of flowers or had an interest in florigraphy. References to floral meanings are rare in his letters, and many of the flowers he chose for his bouquets, such as pansies and zinnias, had no specific meaning in the French guides. It seems more likely that Vincent arranged his bouquets of flowers purely for their visual effects.

The observation of nature

In his quest to improve his painting by concentrating on bouquets as a subject, Vincent was linked to tradition in another, highly significant way. The lifelike appearance of Netherlandish still-life painting derived from the artists' skill and their meticulous observation of the subject. This practice of attentive visual investigation had its origins in the scientific theories of English philosopher Francis Bacon (1561–1626), who asserted that the key to knowledge was the close surveillance of the visible world. The still-life painters applied this approach to their art, not only to

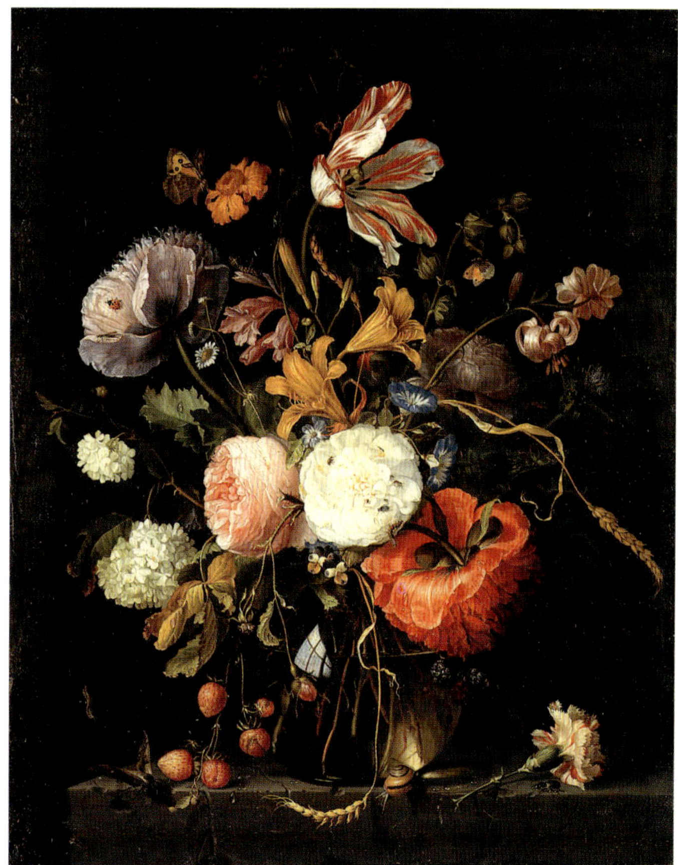

accustom their eye to close observation, but also to train their hand to transcribe exactly what they saw. An amateur naturalist in his youth, Vincent knew the value of close visual attention when studying the natural world. By concentrating on a single subject in his work, he could aspire to translate the knowledge of his observations into the ideas he expressed on his canvas.

But, unlike his Netherlandish predecessors, Vincent did not seek to fool the viewer's eye with visual transcription. Rather, he sought to extrapolate a theory of color based on his close observations of the tones and contrasts that appeared in nature. A letter to his brother, written in the summer of 1886, reveals the importance of color in his artistic conceptions: "As for my work, I painted the pendant to those flowers which you have. A branch of lilies—white, pink, green—against black, something like black Japanese lacquer inlaid with mother-of-pearl, which you know—then a bunch of orange tiger lilies against a blue background, then a bunch of dahlias, violet against a yellow background, and red gladioli in a blue vase against light yellow" (Letter 460).

While Vincent chose backgrounds and containers for his bouquets to heighten the visual interest, his selection of flowers reflects the changing seasons. The vivid purple, blue, and yellow of the pansies he painted, heaped on top of a tambourine, evoke the spirit of spring, while the pale rose and salmon hues contrasted with the dull green of the leaves and stems in *Vase with Autumn Asters*, express the lowering light and cooler atmosphere of autumn. Through painting bouquets in Paris, Vincent explored the ideas he

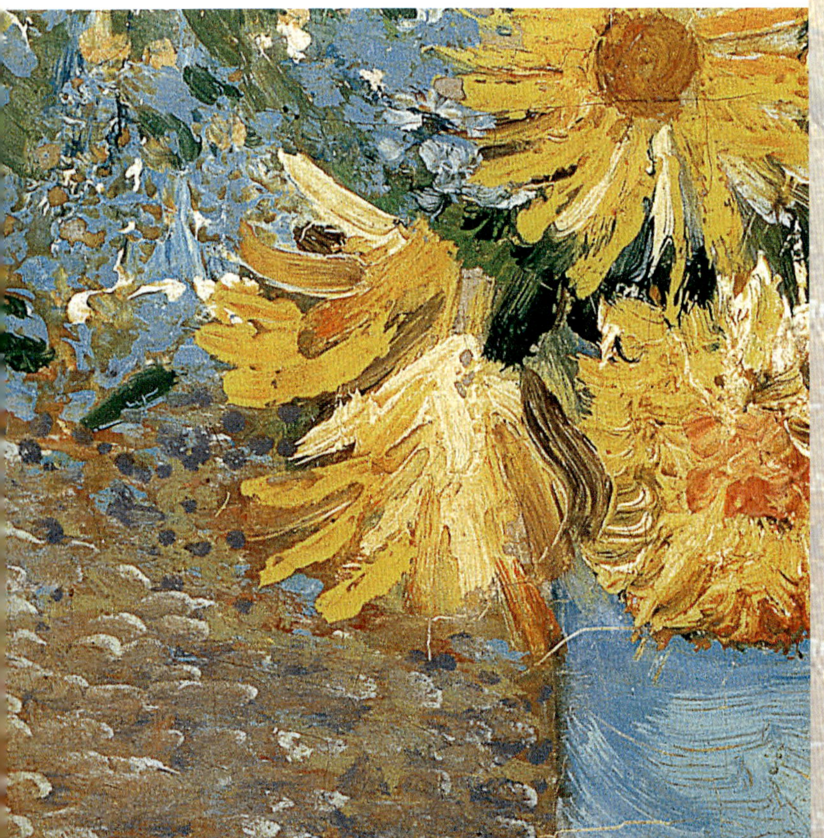

> *"But nevertheless, there is this advantage, there is always something for arranging flowers in or for a still life."*
>
> LETTER TO THEO, JUNE 1890

Flowers in Blue Vase RIGHT AND LEFT
SUMMER 1887. KRÖLLER-MÜLLER MUSEUM, OTTERLO

Vincent painted this exuberant bouquet of daisies and anemones near the end of his stay in Paris. The bright mix of flowers, ranging in hue from deep red-brown to delicate white tinged with pink and pale yellow, gives this work the freshness typical of a traditional nineteenth-century floral still life. But a closer look reveals that Vincent selected these blooms for their broad array of tones within the color yellow. His use of an aqua-blue vase provides a vivid contrast, revealing that he is still fascinated with the idea of color complements, even after experimenting for more than a year. The background, with its broken strokes and dots of color, shows how Vincent brought the techniques of impressionism and divisionism into his work on bouquets.

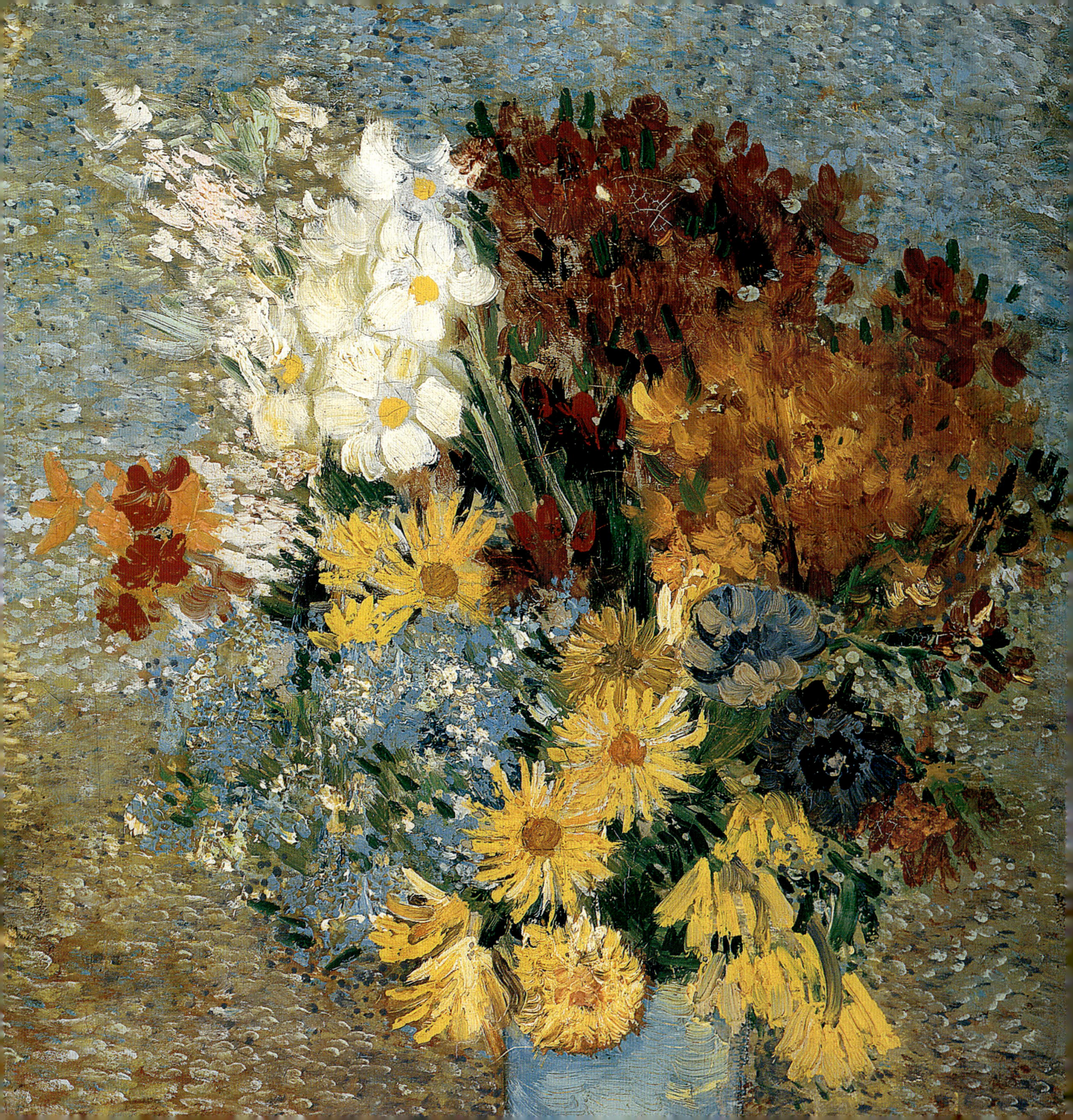

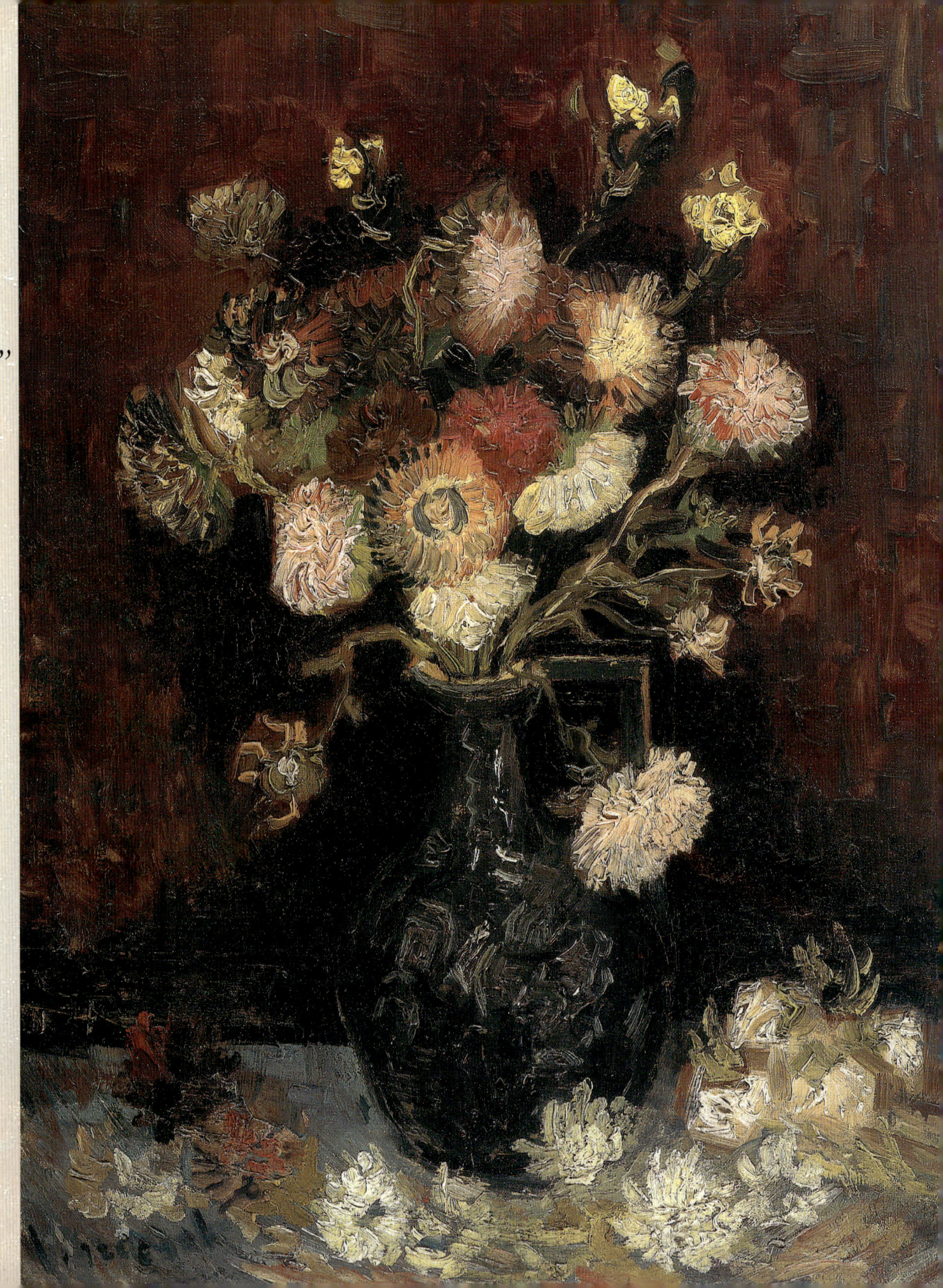

*"In color
seeking life
the true
drawing is
modeling
with color."*

LETTER TO
HORACE LIVENS,
SUMMER 1886

first proposed to his brother in a letter from Nuenen two years earlier, claiming: "one could paint a picture which expressed the mood of the seasons in each of the contrasts of complementary colors" (Letter 372).

Near the end of his first summer in Paris, Vincent wrote a detailed account of his experiences to the English painter Horace Mann Livens, whom he had met during his stay in Antwerp. He states that work is going well, no sales as of yet, but four dealers have exhibited his work and he has exchanged studies with fellow painters. He mentions that much of his time has been devoted to painting bouquets, "I have made a series of color studies in painting, simply flowers, red poppies, blue cornflowers, and myosotis, with rose roses, yellow chrysanthemums—seeking oppositions of blues with orange, red and green, yellow and violet seeking…to render intense color and not a gray harmony" (Letter 459A). While he modestly dismisses this work as "gymnastics," he acknowledges that due to these efforts his command of color in his portraits has greatly improved. Although Vincent continued to paint bouquets well into the following year—and he would return to them as ready models to freshen his palette throughout his career—his Paris flowers taught him to cultivate color in his art.

Vase with Autumn Asters LEFT AND BELOW
AUTUMN 1886. VAN GOGH MUSEUM, AMSTERDAM

In his first six months in Paris, Vincent responded to his exciting new environment through changes in his art. He lightened his palette and worked swiftly with confidence, developing a more spontaneous approach. His touch became subtle and expressive, and he applied his paint freely, achieving a texture as rich as his tone. *Vase with Autumn Asters* marks a synthesis in his Paris period. Working within a close range of pink, rose, red, and brown, Vincent creates a pleasing harmony of color. Pale yellow blossoms, dull green stems, and dabs of blue on the table top provide a subtle contrast. The earthenware jug holding the asters remained in the family and is now in the Van Gogh Museum in Amsterdam.

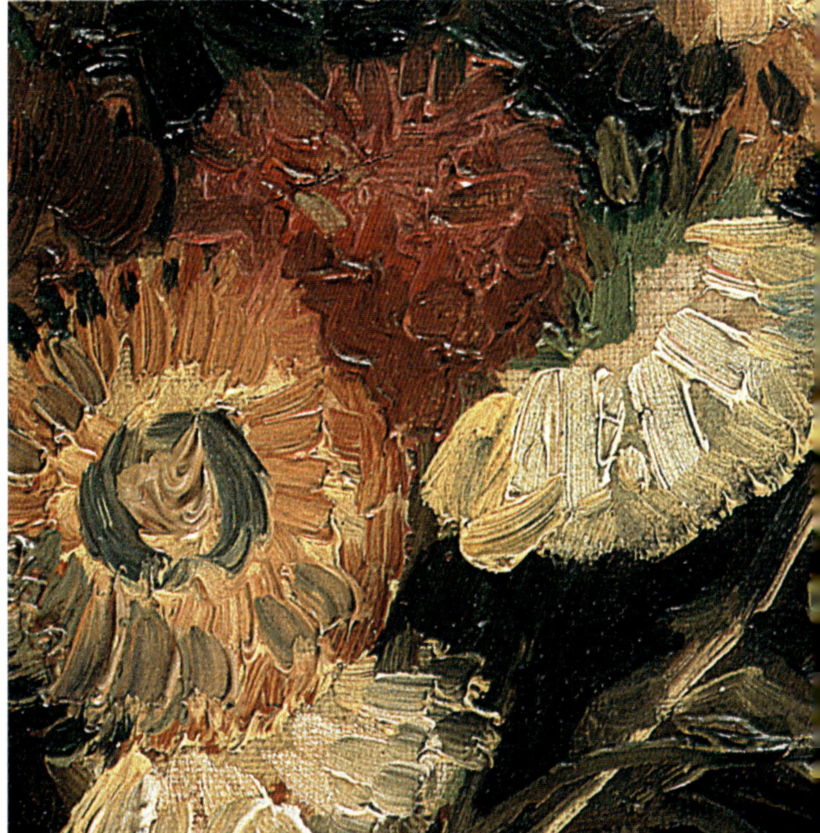

3

Flowering Trees

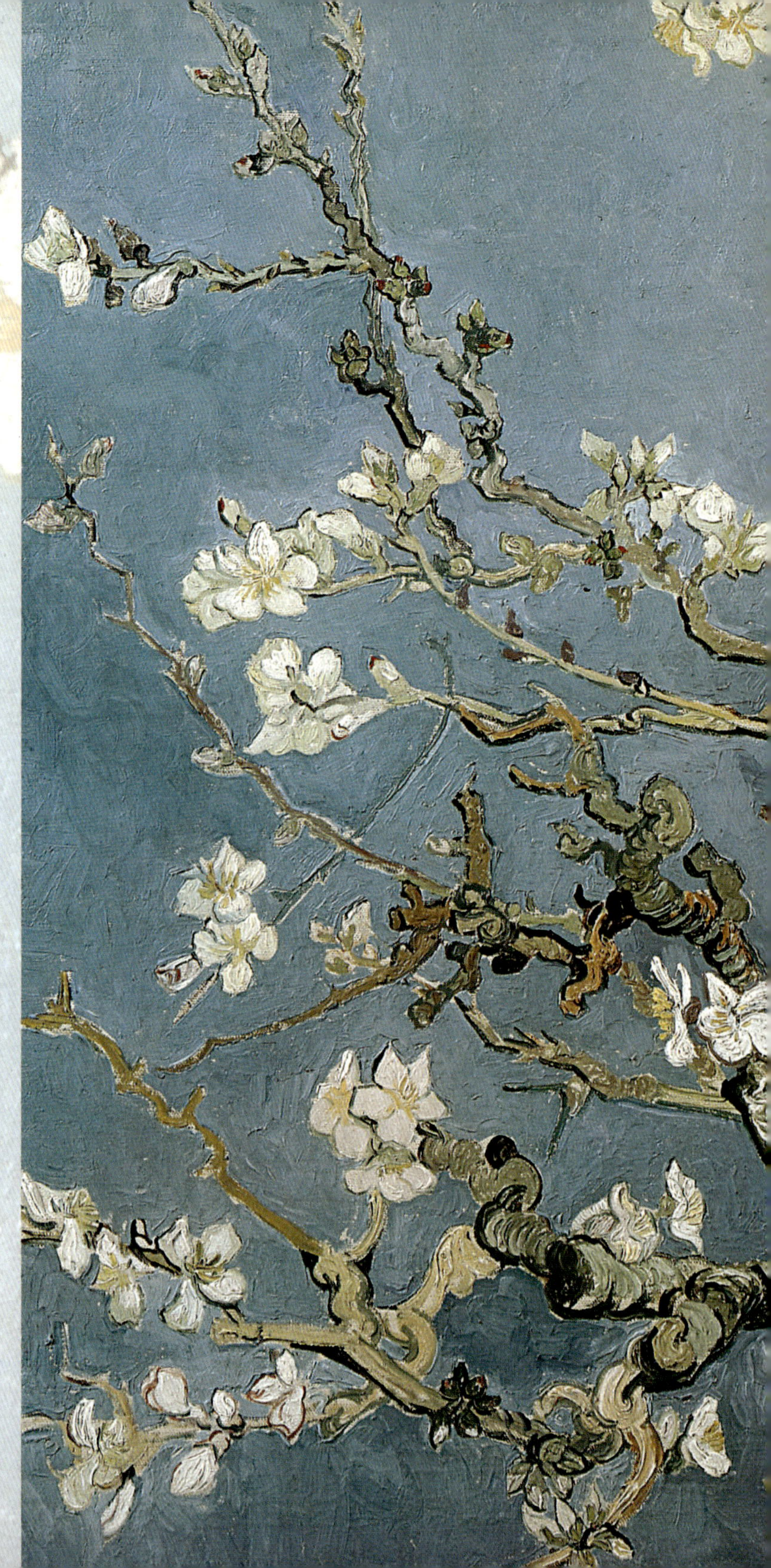

*"Painters understand
nature and love
her and teach us
to see her."*

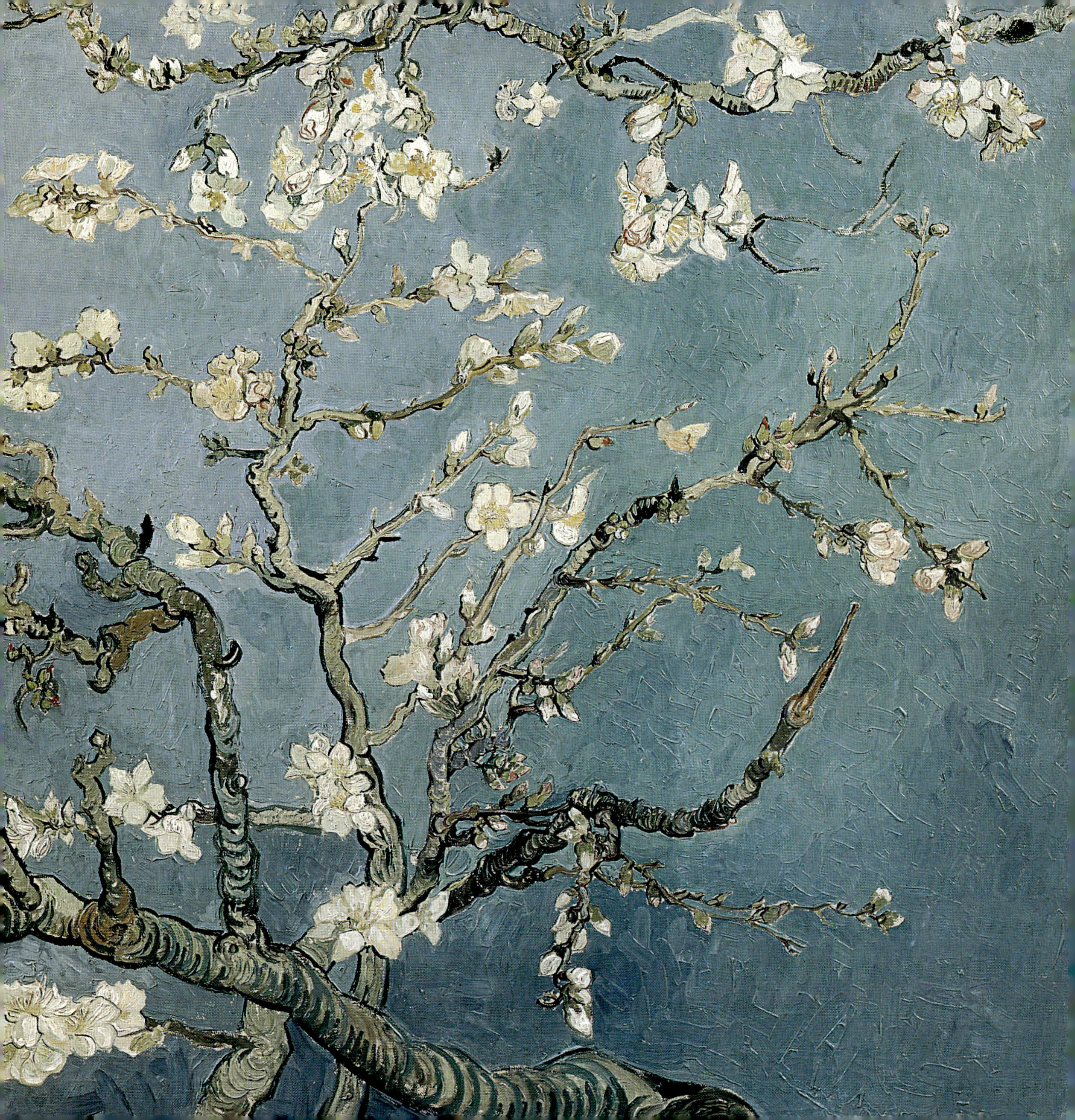

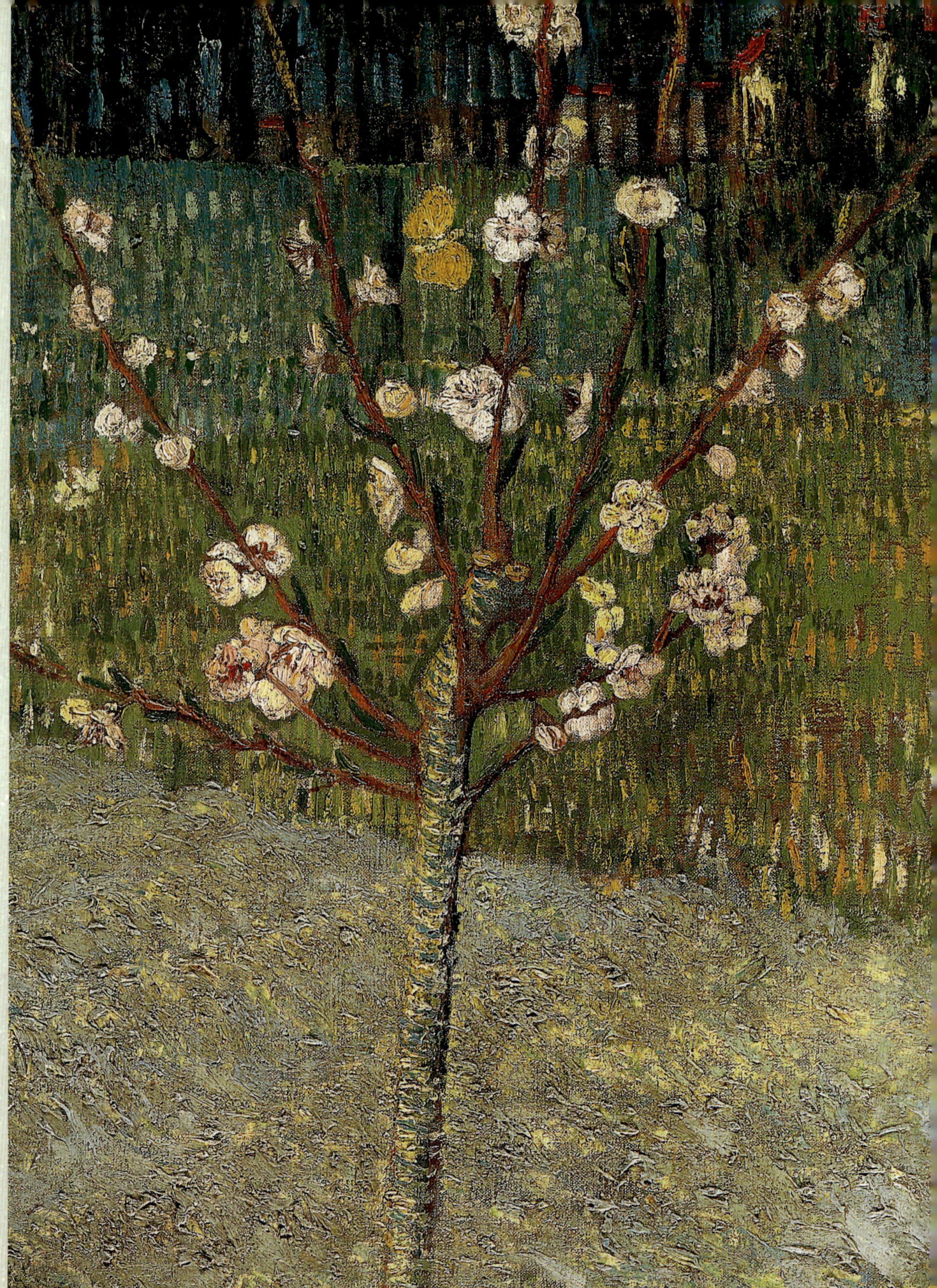

"I am up to
my ears in
work, for
the trees are
in blossom
and I want
to paint a
Provençal
orchard of
astonishing
gaiety."

LETTER TO THEO,
MARCH 1888

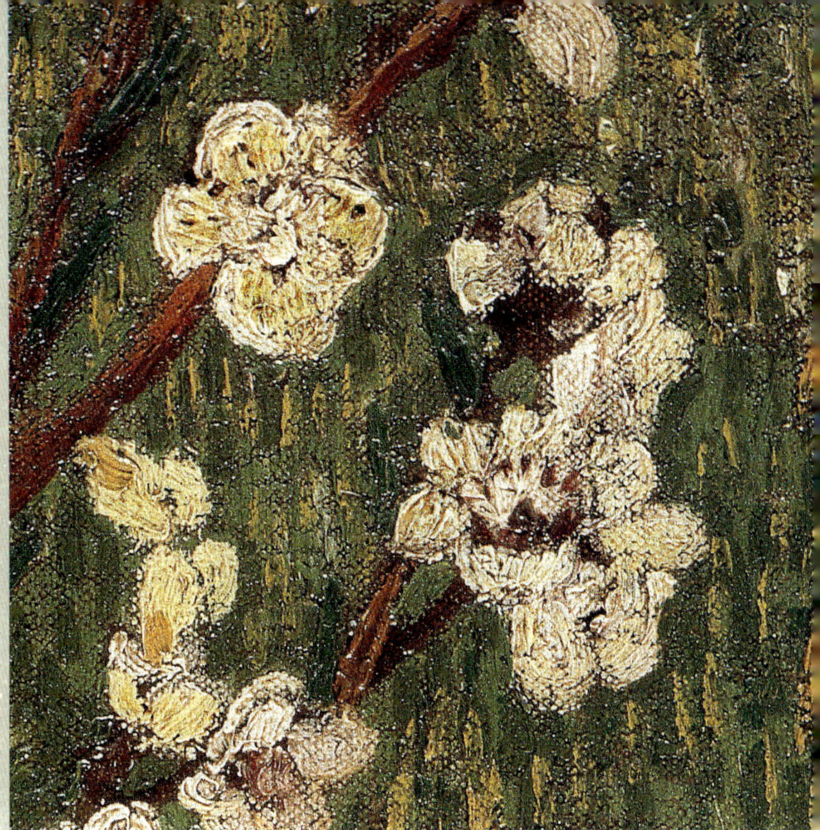

Almond Tree in Blossom LEFT AND RIGHT
APRIL 1888. VAN GOGH MUSEUM, AMSTERDAM

In his flowering trees, Vincent attained a sense of spontaneity, freeing himself from the strict self-analytical approach he took in Paris. In *Almond Tree in Blossom*, Vincent used the light, broken strokes of impressionism and the dabs of color of divisionism for a sparkling surface effect. The distinctive contours of the tree and its position in the foreground recall the formal qualities of Japanese prints.

Almond Blossom PRECEDING PAGES
FEBRUARY 1890. VAN GOGH MUSEUM, AMSTERDAM

Vincent painted this branch of almond blossom in honor of the birth of his nephew, Theo's son, Vincent Willem. The pattern of the limbs and flowers against the bright blue sky reveals that even in his late work, Vincent still sought to instill his art with the simplicity of the Japanese aesthetic. Vincent conveyed the beauty of the tree with just a few random branches, echoing Delacroix's observation that "even a part of a thing is a kind of complete entity in itself."

Vincent's art blossomed in the vital atmosphere of Paris. Always passionate and open-minded, he eagerly observed the work of the most advanced modern painters, and what he saw encouraged him toward his own innovations. In Paris, Vincent brightened his palette, introducing a range of color from shimmering light-struck tones to deep saturated hues. He released his brushwork from its prior rigidity and applied his paint freely, with rhythmic grace and plasticity. Although he once described himself as a painter of ordinary things and working people, he now embraced subjects of contemporary urban life. Most of all, he drew confidence through his participation in this lively environment. After two years in Paris, Vincent had gained a sense of himself as an artist, with a unique vision and a distinctive style.

But what was beneficial for his art proved detrimental to his health. Never able to temper his intense enthusiasm, Vincent suffered from excessive stimulation and his own relentless productivity. The pace of Parisian life exhausted him. Too much drinking and smoking, combined with too little attention to regular meals and rest, made him irritable, excitable, and anxious. Andries Bonger, a friend of Theo, described Vincent's appearance as "sick and emaciated" and suggested that he see a physician. But Vincent knew that his condition depended on more than his physical health. He later wrote to Gauguin that by the end of his stay in Paris he was "seriously sick at heart and in body, and nearly an alcoholic because of my rising fury at my strength failing me" (Letter 544A). During the last months of 1887 a harsh early winter set in, and Vincent began to long for refuge under a warm sun. Late in February 1888 he left Paris for Arles, the capital of Provence.

A friend, Emile Bernard, described Vincent's departure as sudden, but letters reveal that Vincent had been thinking about the move for more than a year. As early as the fall of

1886, he wrote to his friend Livens, "In the spring—say in February or even sooner—I may be going to the South of France, the land of *blue* tones and gay colors." A year later, he expressed the same desire to his sister Wil: "I intend as soon as possible to go temporarily to the South where there is even more color and more sun." Poor health may have prompted him to act more quickly on his long-held desire; he later wrote to Theo that he was in a bad state when he boarded the train, "very miserable, almost an invalid, and almost a drunkard" (Letter 544). But his motivation was less to regain his health than to find new vigor in his art.

For Vincent, the "South" was as much an ideal as a place. In the works of other artists who ventured to southern destinations—Gauguin to Central America, Delacroix to North Africa—he detected a vitality and power that he attributed to the climate. Vincent may have chosen Arles rather than a more distant and exotic locale in regard to his

The Plum Tree Teahouse at Kameido, **Utagawa Hiroshige** RIGHT 1857. VAN GOGH MUSEUM. AMSTERDAM

The Flowering Plum Tree (after Hiroshige) FAR RIGHT SUMMER 1887. VAN GOGH MUSEUM. AMSTERDAM

Based on Hiroshige's *The Plum Tree Teahouse at Kameido,* Vincent's *The Flowering Plum Tree* is believed to be the first of the three oil copies he made of Japanese prints. His handling of color, from the bright, yet modulated reds and greens of the background to the delicate, green tinge in the white blossoms, reveals how he tried to emulate the effects of printer's ink in oil. After his arrival in Arles he wrote to his sister Wil that he no longer needed to study Japanese prints, "because I am always telling myself *that here I am in Japan.*"

health, but the Provençal region had important associations for him. Paul Cézanne, Emile Zola, and the flower painter Adolphe Monticelli all came from the South of France.

"Nature under a brighter sky"

Never having been to Arles, Vincent pictured it as a French equivalent to the world he saw in Japanese prints: clear atmosphere and blooming trees, with the local people living in harmony with nature. He went to Arles "to see a different light…nature under a brighter sky" (Letter 605). But most of all, he sought a renewal, for his art as well as his life. In departing Paris for Arles, he left the artificial environment of the city to seek the authenticity of nature manifest in an early spring.

As Vincent's train reached Arles on February 20, he was surprised to see the surrounding countryside blanketed in snow. Although spring seemed as distant as it did in Paris, Vincent noticed a greater subtlety of color in Provence. In a letter to Theo he noted mountains "of the most delicate lilac" which set off "the landscapes in the snow, with the summits white against the sky as luminous as the snow" (Letter 463). Within a few days he wrote to tell his brother that he had found lodgings and a place to buy art materials. He also sent Theo news of his health: "My blood is actually beginning to think of circulating, which is more than it ever did during that last period in Paris" (Letter 464).

In the first week of March the weather remained bitterly cold. When Vincent attempted to paint "snowscapes" he found the work too arduous. But as he explored Arles, he noticed fresh green buds on the almond trees. He broke off a twig and placed it in a glass of water in his room. There, he painted two small studies of the little branch as it came into full flower. In the white petals, tipped with tints of delicate pink and pale yellow, Vincent saw the promise of the spring to come.

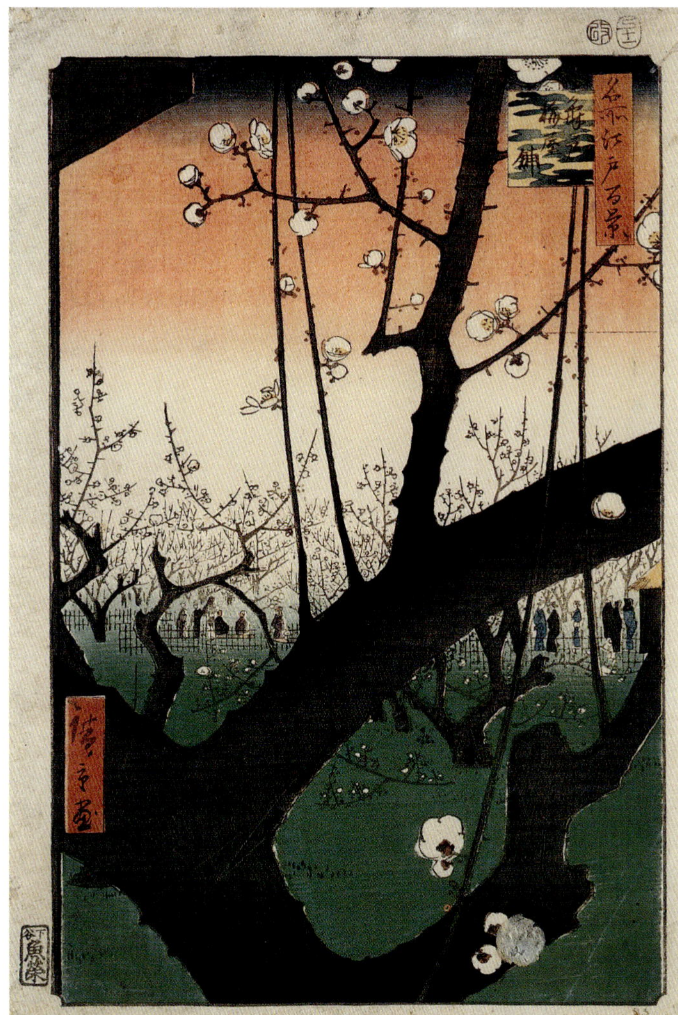

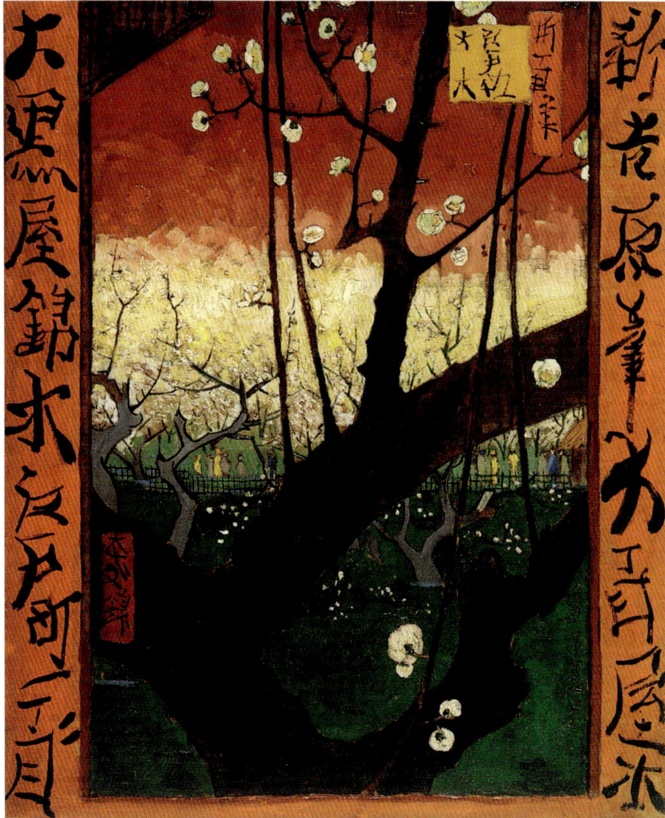

As the month progressed, the trees began to bloom. Among the first was the peach tree; the almond tree followed, with pale pink flowers that turned white even before the tender first leaves appeared on the branches. By the end of the month, all the fruit trees in the orchards—plum, apricot, pear, apple, and cherry—were either budding or in full blossom. After painting bouquets in the confines of his studio in Paris, Vincent was captivated by the delicate yet vital spectacle of spring in Provence. Day after day he set up his easel in the orchards, working rapidly to capture the transient beauty of the annual flowering of the trees. From the end of March through April, he painted in a state he called *un rage de travail* (a frenzy of work), for as he explained to Theo, "There is nothing like striking while the iron is hot" (Letter 474).

The beauty of the orchards in bloom shook Vincent out of his torpor, and he worked with direction and energy, completing more than twenty paintings before the trees dropped their blossoms. To take best advantage of his time, he worked on several canvases at once. Letters to Bernard, Theo, and Wil record his intense involvement and rapid production, and the number of simultaneous studies grew as the season progressed. On March 30, he had six canvases started, and by the third week of April he was working on as many as nine. At the end of the month he wrote to his brother: "I now have ten orchards, three small studies, and in addition to these, a large one of a cherry orchard that I botched" (Letter 478).

Vincent also found that working in the open air restored his health and sense of well-being. He wrote to Theo that breathing the country air was so stimulating that he no longer required alcohol; in fact, he confessed, even a small glass of brandy was enough to make him drunk. In contrast to the exhaustion brought on by earlier periods of intense activity, Vincent was now invigorated. Allowing the season's cycle to set his working rhythm, he felt in harmony with his surroundings. Painting his vision of a southern spring lifted his spirits, and his joyous mood matched the bright promise of nature's annual rebirth. He wrote, "I am up to my ears in work, for the trees are in blossom and I want to paint a Provençal orchard of astonishing gaiety" (Letter 473).

An artistic vision

Working in the orchards outside of Arles, Vincent felt a release from the constraints of Paris. In his new life in the south, he began to recover from the ill effects of his urban claustrophobia and the bleak oppression of a damp, northern winter. But more importantly, Vincent gained confidence in his own artistic vision and power, drawing his inspiration from the harmony he felt with his new surroundings. His struggle with his art seemed, for now, to have passed, and he told his sister Wil, "I have only to open my eyes and paint what is in front of me, if I think it effective." Trusting his own instincts, Vincent abandoned his self-conscious practice of incorporating the technical features of styles he admired into his own. "My brush stroke has no system at all," he exclaimed in a letter to Bernard in April. To capture the vital effects of pink peach trees and pale yellow pear

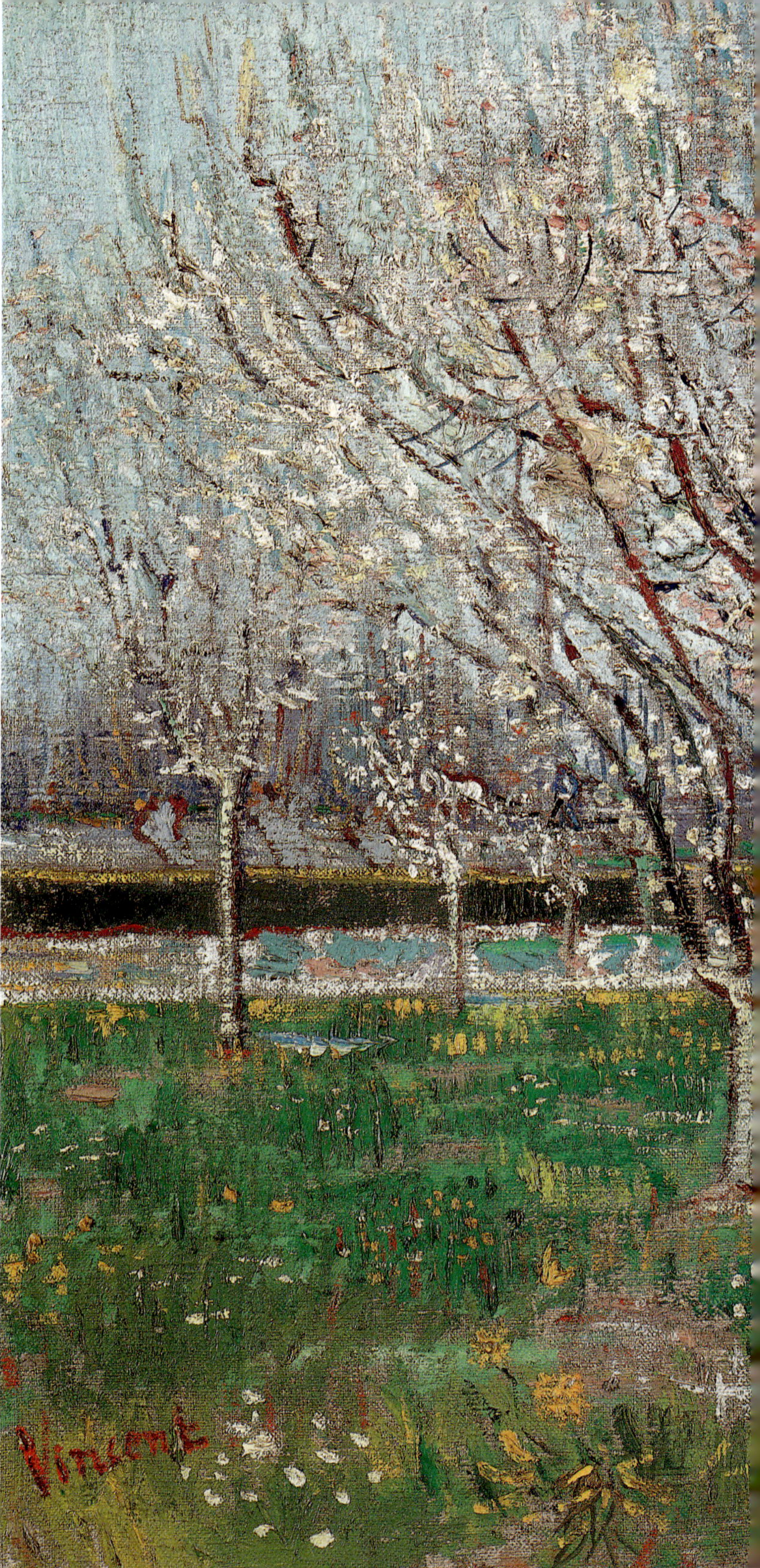

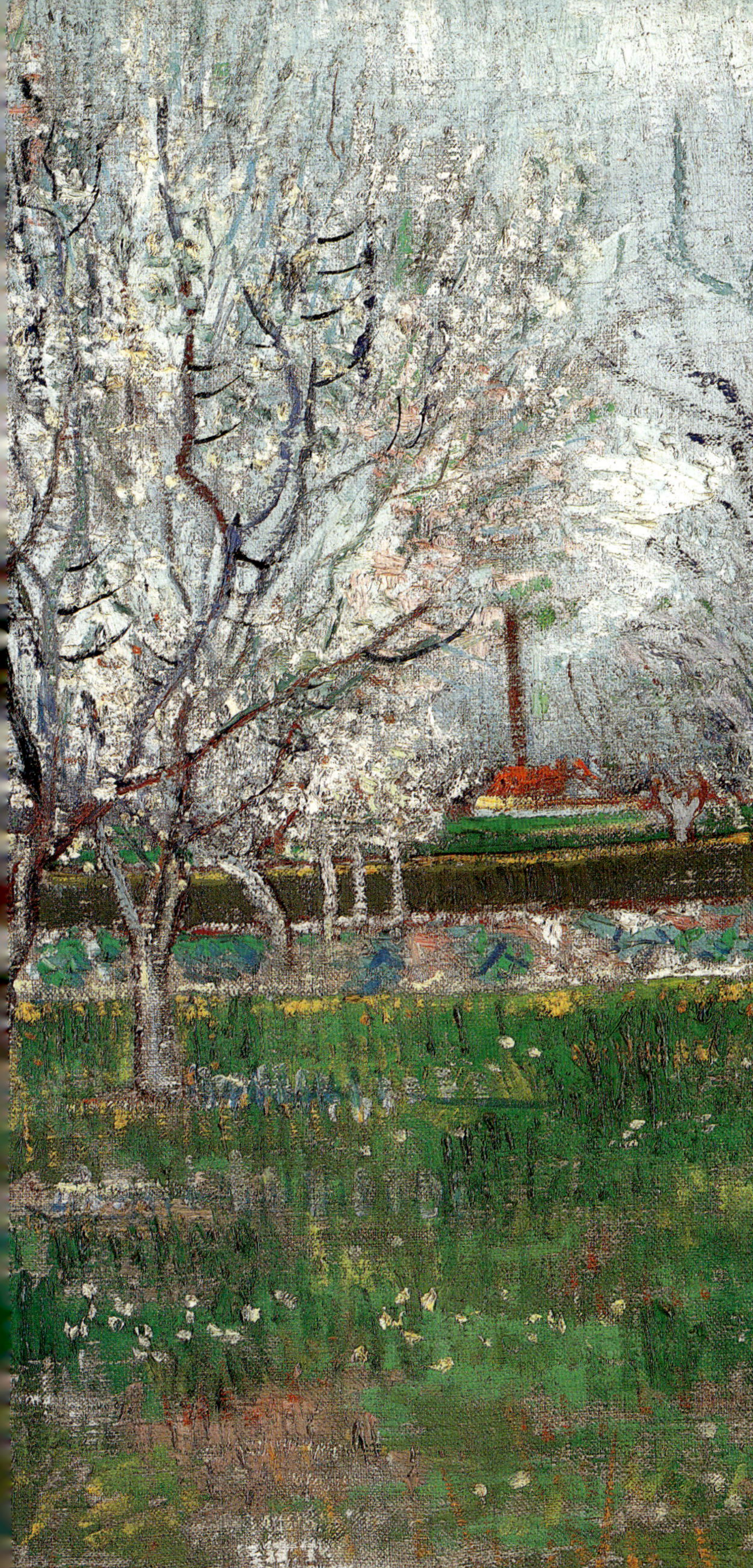

*"I worked on an
orchard of plum trees
in bloom…and all
the little white
flowers sparkled."*

Orchard in Blossom (detail)
APRIL 1888. NATIONAL GALLERY OF SCOTLAND

Blossoms appear on the knotted branches of plum trees in advance
of the first spring leaves. The petals are greenish-white when they
bloom; they brighten to a purer white and then fade into tints of
pink and rose before they fall. The glittering white blossoms, as
well as the absence of leaves, reveal that Vincent painted *Orchard in
Blossom* shortly after the trees flowered. He described the subject to
Theo: "At the moment I am working on some plum trees, yellowish-
white, with thousands of black branches." While his words evoke the
Japanese print by Hiroshige that inspired his *Flowering Plum Tree* of
the previous year, Vincent painted these trees in an impressionist
manner, using a flickering stroke and natural effects of light.

Pink Peach Trees RIGHT AND BELOW
MARCH 1888. KRÖLLER-MÜLLER MUSEUM, OTTERLO

To capture the delicate blossoms of the peach trees, Vincent worked rapidly, his brush strokes flickering like petals in the wind. While working on this painting, Vincent received the news of Anton Mauve's death and in his memory signed the work "Souvenir de Mauve, Vincent." He explained to his sister Wil that the delicate palette expressed his fond, but poignant response to his loss: "It seemed to me that everything in memory of Mauve must be at once tender and very gay, and not a study in a graver key."

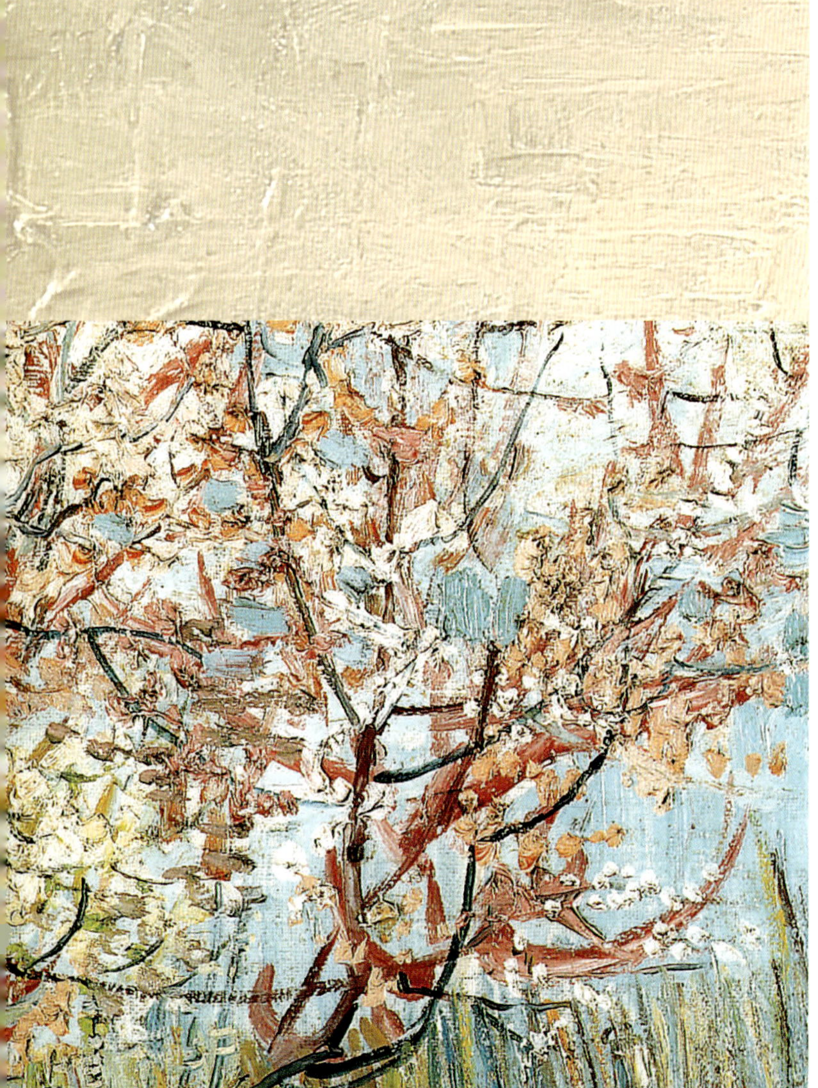

trees in blossom, Vincent worked freely, relying upon his immediate response to what he observed. He applied his paint thickly, leaving patches of the canvas uncovered, and reflected with delight how the "savageries" of his new style of painting would be "so disquieting and irritating as to be a godsend to those who have fixed preconceived ideas about technique."

Of all his pictures of flowering trees, Vincent took the greatest pleasure in painting *Pink Peach Trees*. Perhaps he was deeply inspired by the exquisite sight of "pink against a scintillating blue sky with white clouds," for he confessed to Theo that it was painted "with a sort of passion." While working on this and several other studies of peach trees, Vincent received a memorial tribute, sent by his sister Wil, on the life of Anton Mauve, who had died in February. Reading it, Vincent remembered Mauve's kind interest in his work during his stay in The Hague. They had disagreed on many issues, but Vincent never forgot how Mauve had encouraged him to work in color. He asked Theo to send the fresh, bright painting of the peach tree to Mauve's widow Jet, explaining that when he read the tribute, he felt a profound sense of loss. This moved him to inscribe the canvas "Souvenir de Mauve, Vincent."

Throughout the month of April, Vincent spent his days in the orchards. Even the fierce winds that occasionally swept the countryside failed to deter him. He concentrated his efforts during the sunny intervals, working in the groves of plum trees where "the little white flowers sparkled." As with the peach trees, he made several studies of each subject, and he noted to Theo that as he completed his individual canvases, he would come back to them and touch them up to "give them a certain unity." In a letter written on April 20, he happily informed Theo that ten of his orchard paintings, along with his depiction of the bridge at the Pont de l'Anglais (*The Bridge at Langlois*), would constitute

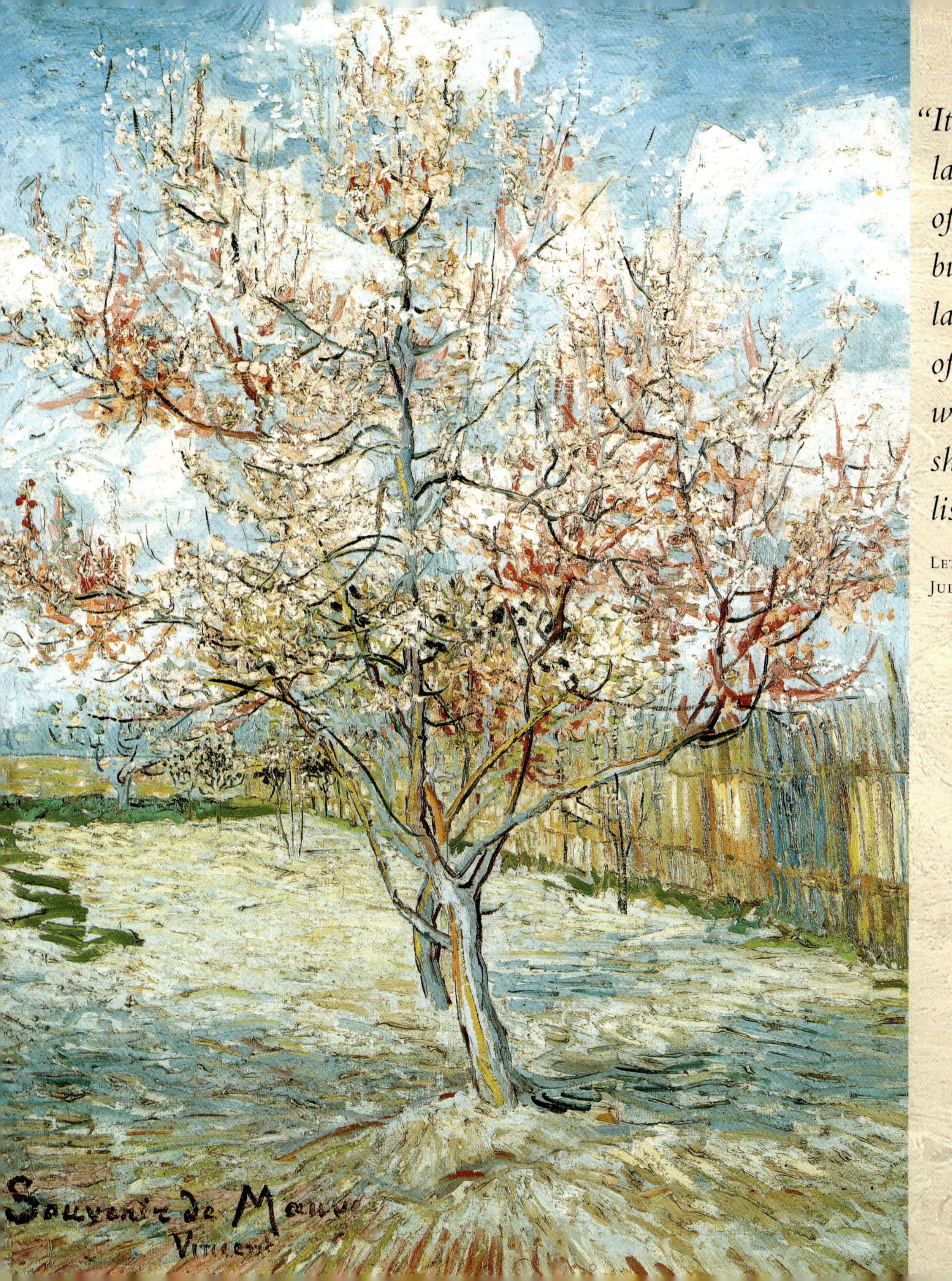

"It is not the language of painters but the language of nature which one should listen to."

Letter to Theo, July 1882

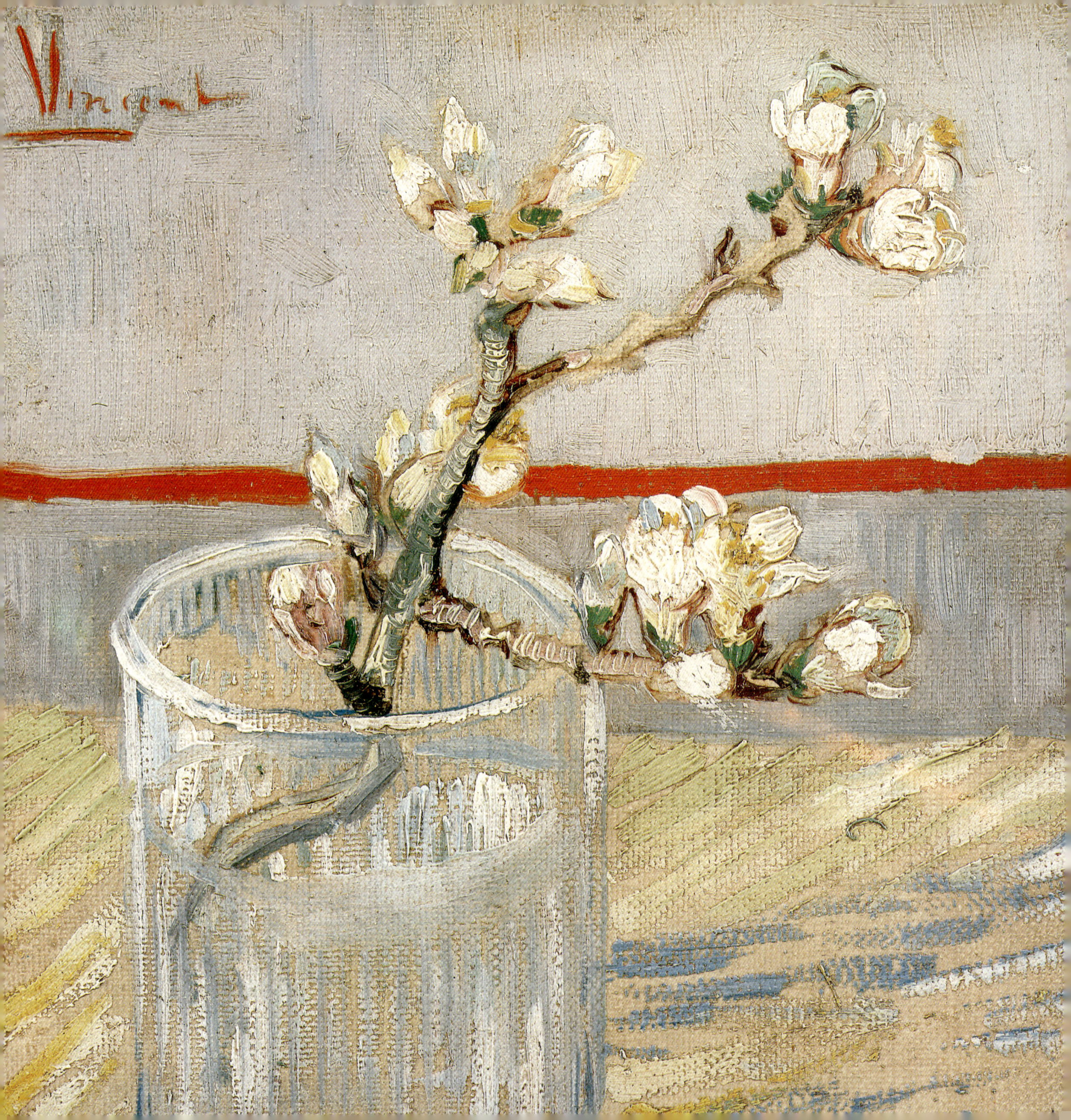

Vincent

his first series in Arles. Although he may have been thinking of the sequential approach taken by Claude Monet in his depictions of the Palace of Westminster (1870–71) and of the Gare Saint-Lazare (1874–76), Vincent conceived his series with an essential difference. Monet returned to his subject at different times of the day to record the varied light effects; later, in the 1890s, he would take the same approach to capture seasonal changes, using rural subjects such as grain stacks. Rather than selecting a static subject which reflected the mutability of light and atmosphere, Vincent chose the blossoming orchard trees, which were themselves subject to natural change. Unlike Monet, who depicted nature selectively to study temporal effects, Vincent embraced nature collectively, allowing the alterations inherent to his subject's lifecycle to shape his sequence.

In choosing to let nature set the rhythm for his work, Vincent recognized that his series of flowering trees faced an inevitable end. Late in April he wrote anxiously to Theo to request more paint and canvas. He was working at a furious pace, explaining to his brother that "The flowering time is over so soon" (Letter 475). But Vincent also remained painfully aware of his own restless nature, reminding Theo, "You know I am changeable in my work, and this craze for painting orchards will not last for ever" (Letter 474). In mid-May, as the temperature rose and the blossoms began to drop from the branches, Vincent's interest turned to the flowers blooming in the fields, but he promised Theo that he would undertake a new and larger series of orchards in next year's season. Even after the onset of his illness, Vincent held out hope that he could revive his sense of purpose by painting the flowering trees. On January 1, 1889, he shared with his brother a guarded, but optimistic plan: "Soon the fine weather will be coming and I shall again start on the orchards in bloom" (Letter 566). However, his repeated periods in hospital made that impossible.

In the following February, as a resident in Saint-Rémy, Vincent received the happy news that Theo's wife Jo had given birth to a healthy son on January 31. As a gift to the boy, who was named Vincent Willem after him, Vincent painted the twisting branch of an almond tree, its delicate flowers sparkling against a bright blue sky. The greenish tinge of the bark, the white blossoms, and the absence of leaves reveal that this branch has just begun to flower. For Vincent, a tree in bloom was nature's cycle made manifest, and he celebrated the birth of his nephew by painting his personal emblem of rebirth and spring.

Sprig of Flowering Almond in a Glass
FEBRUARY–MARCH 1888. VAN GOGH MUSEUM, AMSTERDAM

When Vincent arrived in Provence, he was surprised to find the branches of the fruit trees bare and stark under the wintry skies. Noticing that the buds on an almond tree seemed ready to burst into flower, he broke off a twig and brought it into blossom in a glass of water. Vincent painted two studies of the branch of almond blossom. In this tiny painting, he used light strokes and delicate tints to convey the first fragile signs of spring.

4
Irises

"I study nature, so as not to do foolish things, to remain reasonable."

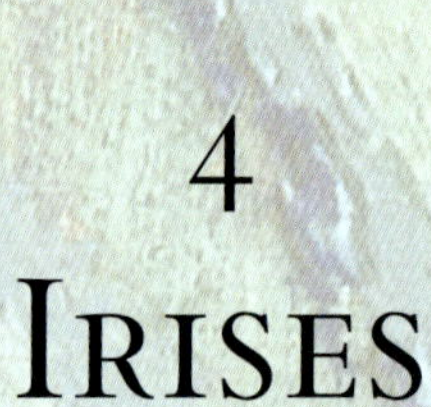

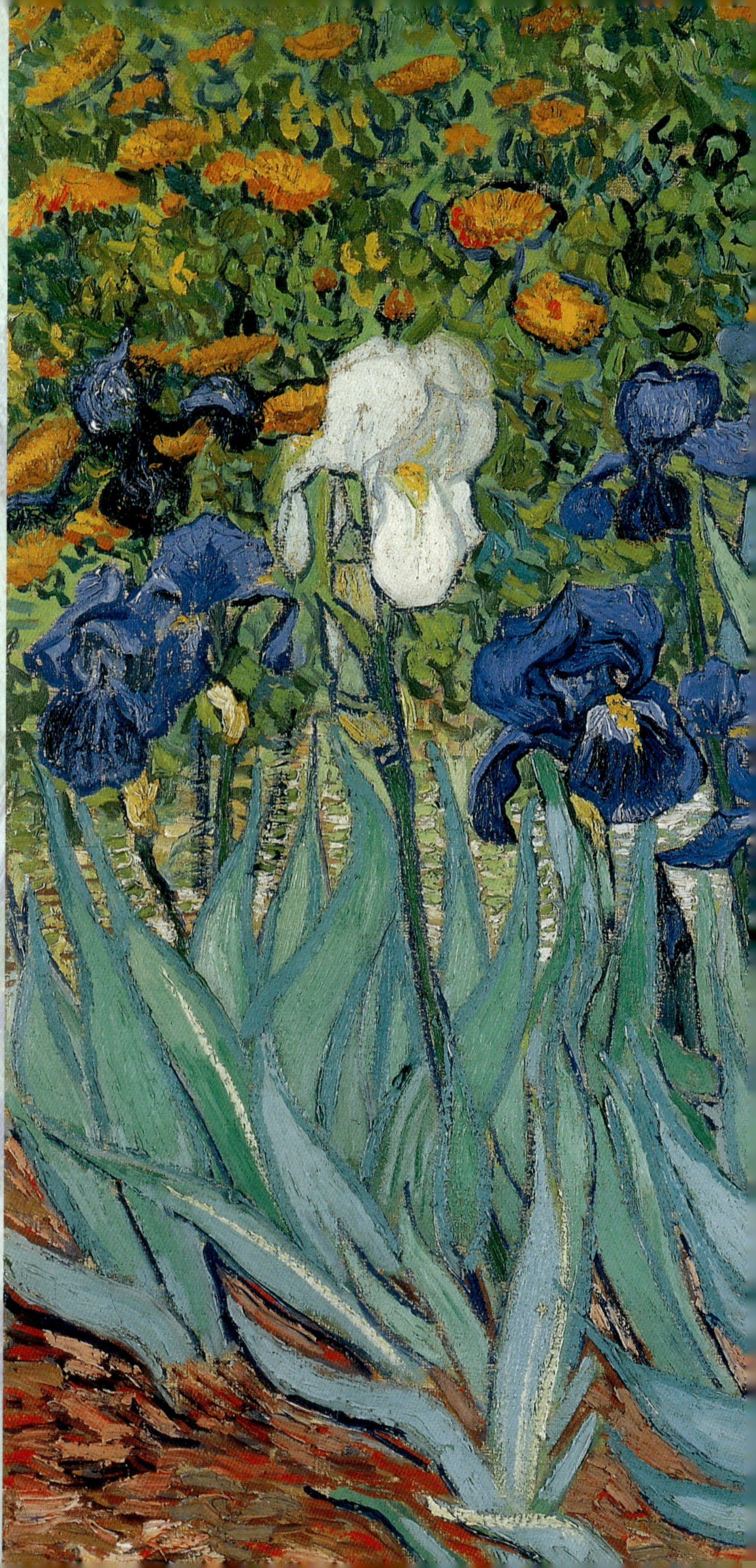

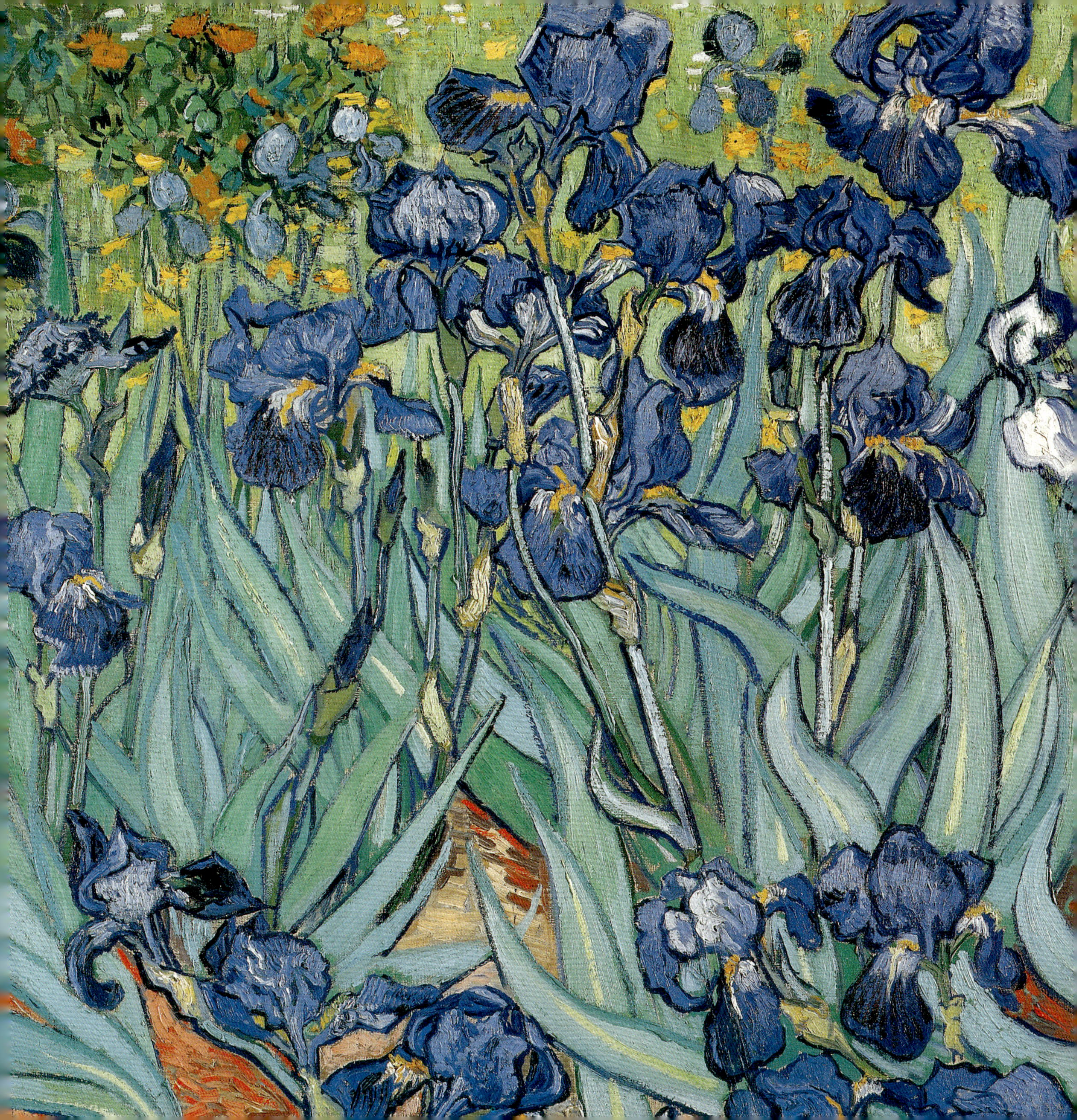

The Café Terrace at Night, "Place du Forum," Arles
RIGHT AND BELOW
SEPTEMBER 1888. KRÖLLER-MÜLLER MUSEUM, OTTERLO

In the late summer and autumn of 1888, Vincent found new subjects in Arles. The effects of the gas-lit square he portrayed in *The Café Terrace*, illuminated with a "pale sulfur and greenish citron-yellow color," intrigued him. He described this work to his sister Wil as a "night picture without any black in it," painted in "beautiful blue and violet and green." He worked spontaneously, setting up his easel in the street, and confided to Wil, "It amuses me enormously to paint the night right on the spot."

Irises PRECEDING PAGES
MAY 1889. GETTY MUSEUM, MALIBU

Vincent's room in the asylum of Saint-Rémy overlooked the unkempt garden, where wild flowers bloomed. Using a room on the first floor as a studio, Vincent painted a patch of irises that grew among the weeds. He reassured Theo that he was adjusting to life in the asylum: "When you receive the canvases I have done in the garden, you will see that I am not too melancholy here" (Letter 593).

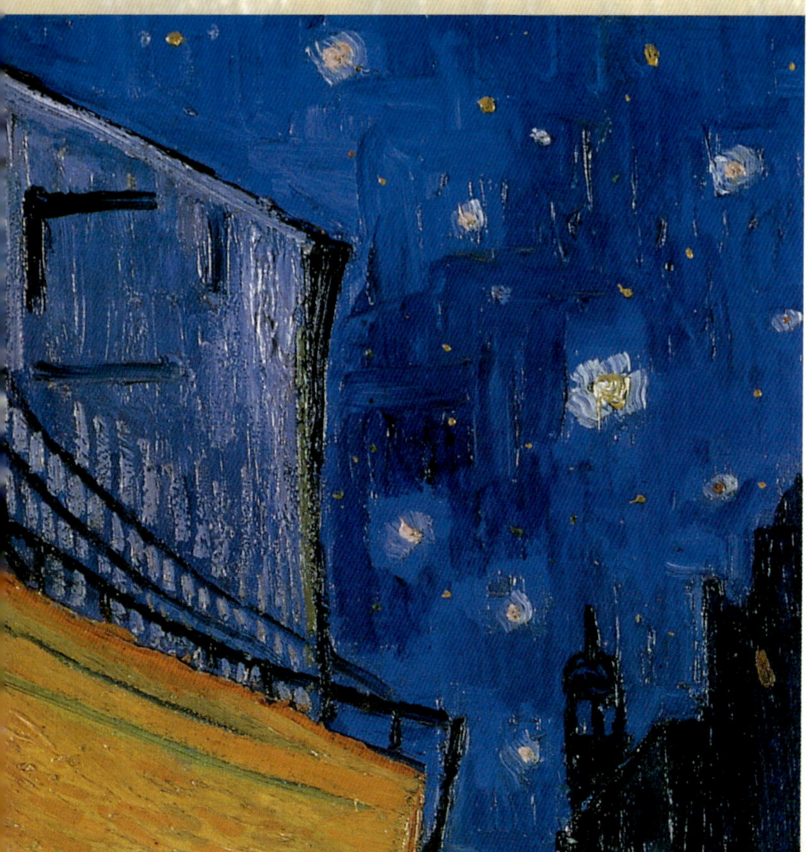

By mid-May, the strengthening sun heated the air and summer bloomed in the Provençal countryside. Vincent watched the delicate blossoms fall from the flowering trees with some regret, but the changing weather also delighted him. Throughout his stay in Paris he had longed for the warmth and high colors of the south, and his first summer in Arles more than met his expectations. In his many walks outside the city, he observed the green meadows bursting into a colorful blaze of glory: bright wild flowers under the intensifying sun.

Eager to sustain his artistic link to the seasons, Vincent altered his palette; the delicate tints he used to capture the transient beauty of the blooming orchards in spring gave way to stronger tones and bolder contrasts. As he roamed the countryside searching for subjects, his excitement grew, as did his joy in experiencing summer in Provence. Vincent wrote to his friend Emile Bernard that Arles was a painter's paradise: "The town is surrounded by immense meadows all abloom with countless buttercups—a sea of yellow—in the foreground these meadows are divided by a ditch full of violet irises." With nature to guide him, he marveled at how life and art seemed in perfect sympathy: "What a subject, hein! That sea of yellow with a band of violet irises, and in the background that coquettish little town of the pretty women!"

Emboldened with new spirit, Vincent expanded his repertoire. He painted the flowering meadows, and when the farmers mowed the fields, he portrayed them at their labors. He depicted women washing their clothes on the riverbank, with a farm wagon trundling over the bridge above them. With greater confidence, he sought out scenes in the city, painting the houses, streets, and cafés. He also painted portraits of his new acquaintances in Arles—the soldier Milliet, a second lieutenant of the Zouaves, and the postal worker Joseph Roulin and his family.

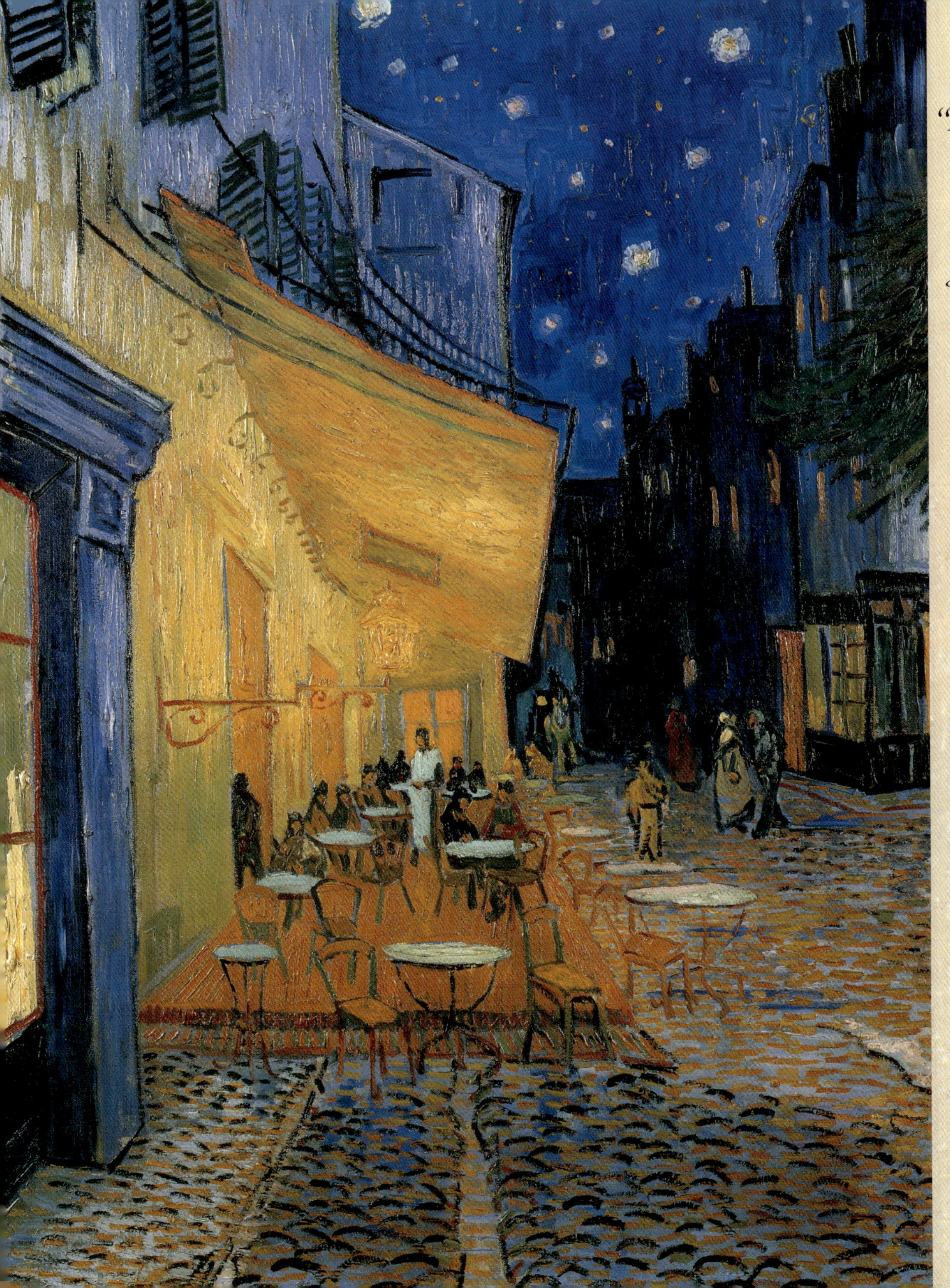

"A café, with
the terrace lit
up by a big
gas lamp in
the blue night,
and a corner
of a starry
blue sky."

LETTER TO THEO,
SEPTEMBER 1888

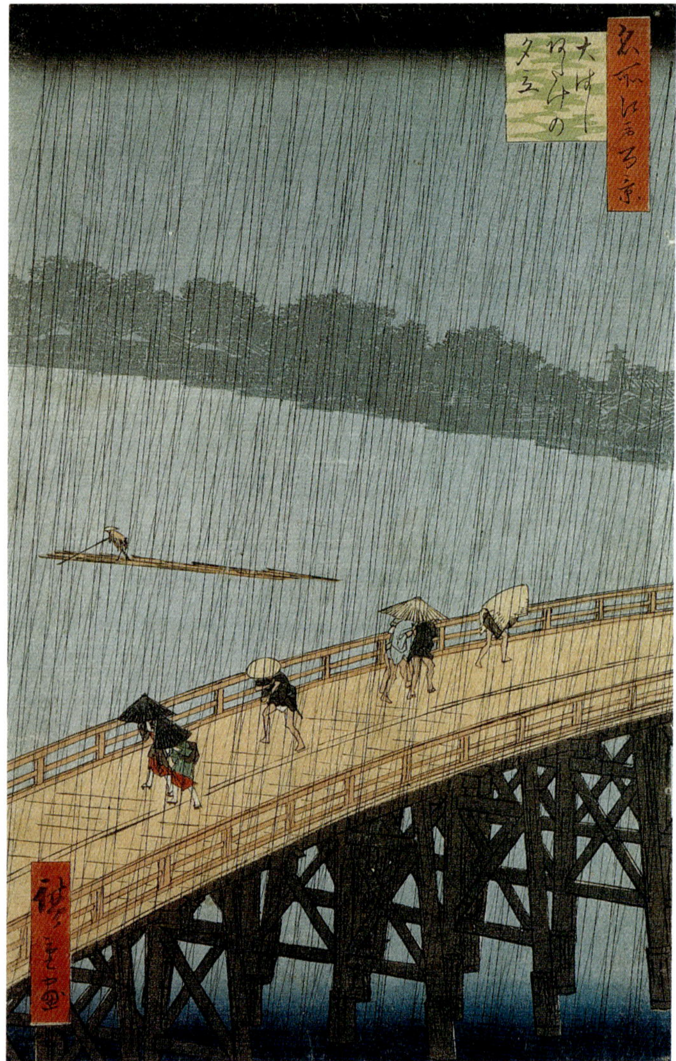

The Bridge in the Rain (after Hiroshige) RIGHT
SUMMER 1887. VAN GOGH MUSEUM, AMSTERDAM

Sudden Shower on the Great Bridge, Utagawa Hiroshige LEFT
1857. VAN GOGH MUSEUM, AMSTERDAM

Hiroshige (1797–1858) was one of the last great masters of the *Ukiyo-e* in Japan and earned his reputation with series of views featuring the well-known sights of Japan. Vincent copied Hiroshige's print *Sudden Shower on the Great Bridge* to study the visual effects of the *Ukiyo-e* aesthetic. He was particularly interested in the formal structure, based on horizontal bands of cool blues and greens, broken only by the foreground diagonal of the yellow bridge. Although Vincent matched his colors to those in the print, he applied his paint with light, short strokes, creating a more vibrant effect than the subtle tones characteristic of the Japanese printing technique. Vincent admired the masterful simplicity and directness of the Japanese art form, exclaiming "I envy the Japanese the extreme clearness which everything has in their work."

Vincent attributed his burst of creative energy to his great love of nature. He also recognized that his current state of productive intensity was as changeable as the passing season: "Is it not emotion, the sincerity of one's feeling for nature, that draws us, and if the emotions are sometimes so strong that one works without knowing one works, when sometimes the strokes come with a continuity and a coherence like words in a speech or a letter, then one must remember that it has not always been so, and that in time to come there will again be hard days, empty of inspiration" (Letter 504). No matter what the subject, he expressed his passionate appreciation of his surroundings in the colors of Provence, the strong contrasts of yellow and blue, that he first saw in the fields of wild irises brightly flowering under the blazing sun.

While Vincent's first Provençal summer satisfied his craving for the color and the warmth of the south, it also fulfilled his long-held dream to discover a real location in which to work that would match his imaginary vision of Japan. He based his idealistic vision of Japanese life upon his own interpretation of Japanese prints. In them, Vincent saw a world of peace and clarity, composed of tranquil landscapes in which men and women carried out their daily tasks with grace and purpose. He firmly believed that the balanced beauty of the Japanese aesthetic reflected a similar balance in the rhythm of life in Japan. In Paris he had longed for a gentler climate, a slower pace of life, and proximity to the rural surroundings that soothed his soul. He chose Arles as a place with the potential to meet these needs. With the right conditions, Vincent believed he could draw inspiration from the calm, quiet existence that he identified as the essence of an artist's life in Japan.

There may have been an arbitrary element in Vincent's insistence that Arles was an apt substitute for the country he knew only through art and imagination. In a letter to Gauguin written in the fall of 1888, he recalled the innocent hopes he carried there. "There is still present in my mind the emotion produced by my own journey from Paris to Arles last winter. How I peered out the window to see whether it was like Japan yet! Childish, wasn't it?" But Japan remained a powerful ideal in his mind, as a place where art, life, and work were at unity with nature.

The art of Japan

For many artists of Vincent's generation, the art of Japan presented an intriguing alternative to conventional western aesthetics. Before the 1850s, Japanese goods rarely appeared in European markets. For centuries, the nation had been closed to foreign trade, barred by the isolationist policy imposed by the Tokugawa shogunate (1597–1867) to preserve cultural purity. In 1853, in an attempt to open up the empire, American naval commander Commodore Matthew Perry anchored his squadron of ships in Tokyo Bay. The following year, backed by the threat of gunboat diplomacy, Perry negotiated a trade treaty and by the end of the decade, Japanese goods flowed into Europe.

While the rare porcelains, painted screens, and textiles appealed to affluent collectors, artists turned their attention to the more affordable prints made by the masters of the *Ukiyo-e* or the "Floating World." The name refers to the

pleasure districts of Edo (present-day Tokyo), but the color wood-block prints featured popular imagery, with subjects ranging from portraits of famous courtesans and theatrical personalities, to notable sights of the countryside and the activities of daily life.

For many artists, the subjects were of less consequence than the formal elements of color and composition in the prints. The flattened perspective, bold hues, and broad areas of pattern suggested a daring alternative to the western approach, in which painting imitated what was perceived

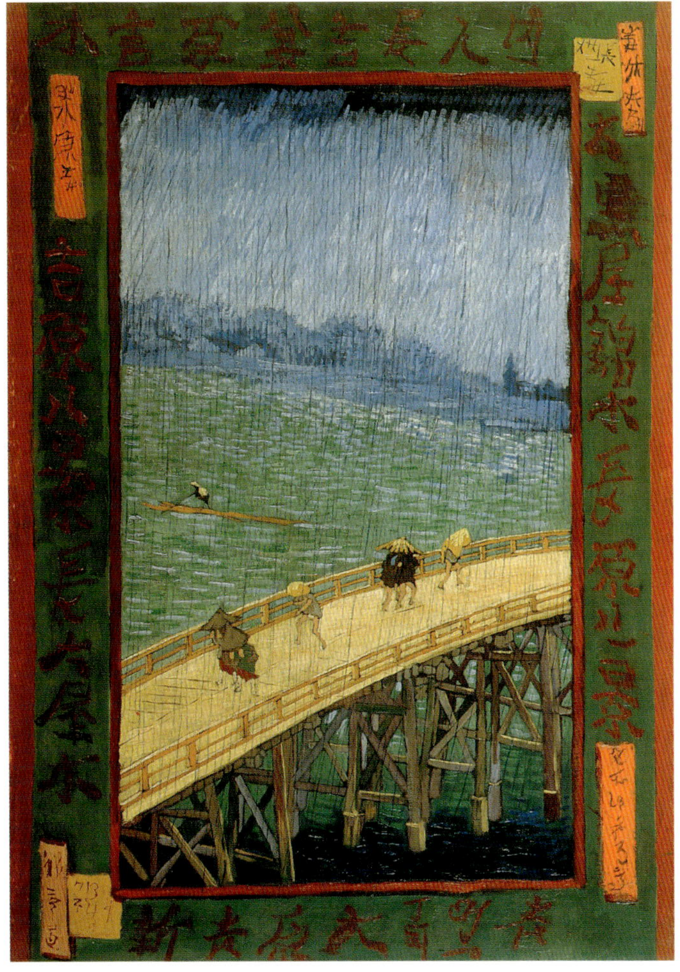

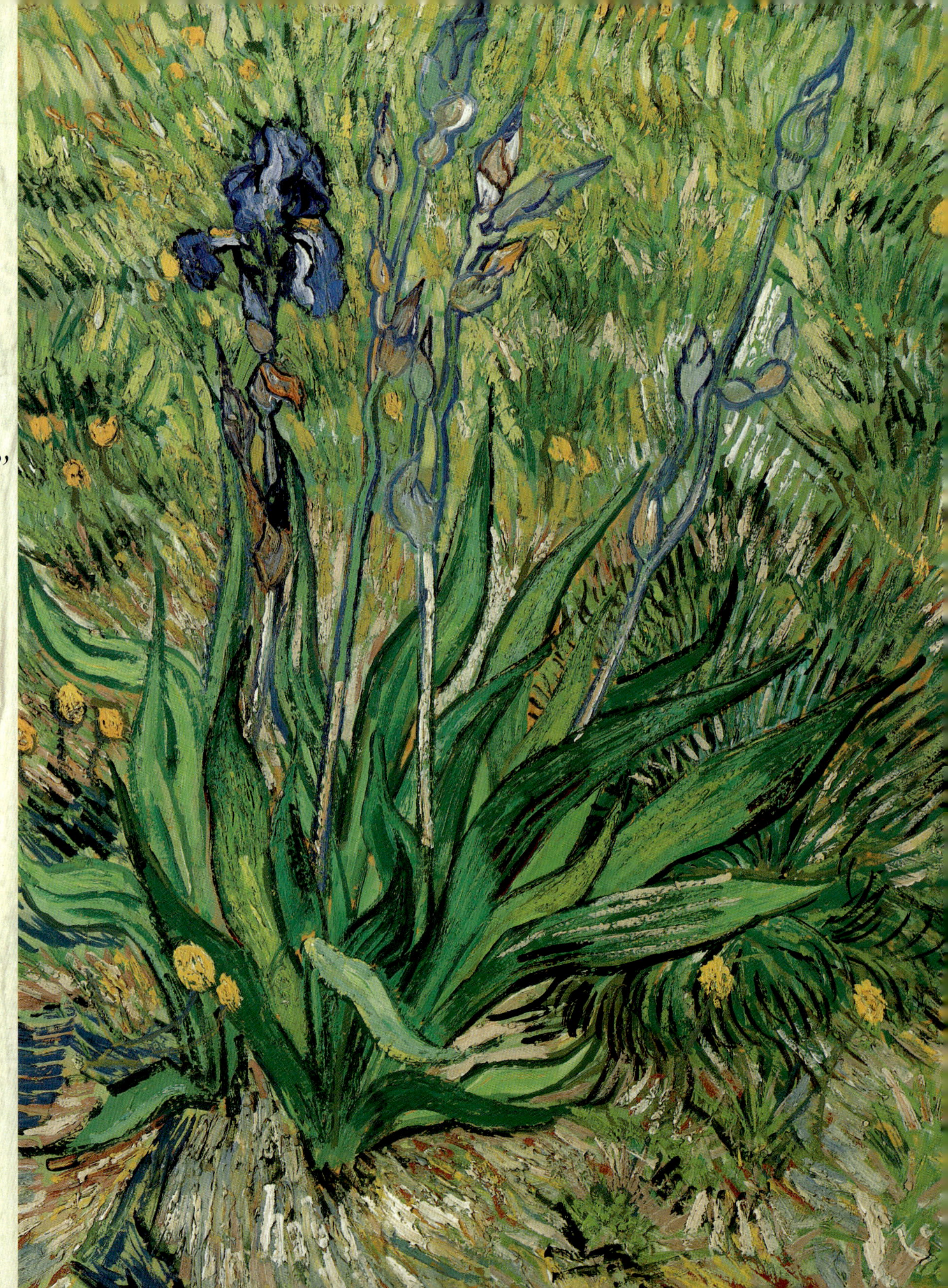

"This is how you must look at Japanese art, in a very bright room, quite bare, and open to the country."

LETTER TO THEO, SUMMER 1888

Iris LEFT

MAY 1889. NATIONAL GALLERY OF CANADA, OTTAWA

Near the end of his first month in residence at Saint-Rémy, Vincent asked Theo to send him more canvas, explaining that it was "just the season when there are plenty of flowers and consequently color effects." In this work, he captured the sinuous vitality of the flower with its single full blossom—sword-shaped petals of bright blue shot with yellow—standing triumphantly above its long, slender leaves and the coarse growth of rough, wild grass.

Irises RIGHT

MAY 1890. THE METROPOLITAN MUSEUM OF ART, NEW YORK

When Vincent painted this bouquet, the joyful exuberance of his first Provençal summer was just a memory, dimmed by the pain and illness that plagued him in his last months in Arles and his time in Saint-Rémy. But he remained certain that through his art he could establish harmony with the natural world and its annual cycle. For Vincent, the iris was both the flower of early summer and the floral emblem of the simple yet eloquent art of Japan.

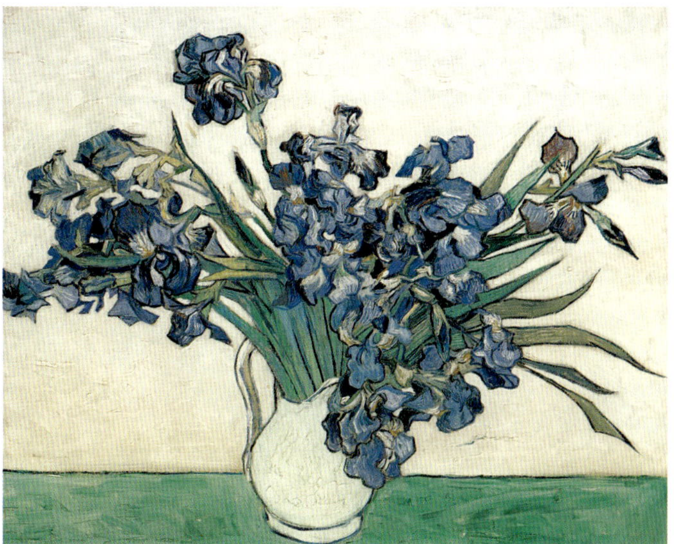

by the human eye. Art critics advocated the appreciation of Japanese art as a model of refinement for European aesthetics. Jules Goncourt, who with his brother Edmond wrote the influential text *L'Art japonais du XVIII siècle*, expressed his passion for Japanese art in a letter written in 1867 that declared "Japonaiserie forever." In 1878, critic Ernest Chesneau offered a more tempered and insightful explanation of the powerful effect the imported works had on contemporary western artists: "What they found in the Japanese was not so much inspiration as the confirmation of their own characters, of their own personal ways of seeing, feeling, understanding things, and entering into the spirit of Nature."

Vincent's own passion for Japanese art first emerged in Antwerp, where in 1885 he had decorated his room with prints he had purchased, and he enthusiastically endorsed Goncourt's credo "Japonaiserie forever" in a letter to Theo.

In Paris, he became an avid collector. Siegfried Bing, a respected dealer in Asian imports whose ample stock was the best in the city, allowed him to browse at his leisure, while Père Tanguy, who traded in prints to supplement his sales of art materials, offered him fair prices. Vincent even organized an exhibition of prints at the Café Tambourin in the spring of 1887. By summer, he was incorporating features of Japanese design in his painting, first decorating frames with Japanese characters and then making copies in oil after his favorite prints.

Vincent also used prints as a decorative and symbolic element in portraiture. For example, a wall covered with Japanese prints provided a backdrop for a portrait Vincent painted of Père Tanguy in the fall of 1887. This not only placed the art dealer in his natural setting, but also served as a way for Vincent to express his admiration for a man he believed had found balance in his work and life.

By the time Vincent traveled to Arles he had a collector's informed knowledge of Japanese art. He had read the Goncourt brothers' pioneering history as well as Bing's study *Le Japon artistique,* which he dismissed as rather dry.

Vincent was particularly taken with *Madame Chrysanthème*, a romantic novel by Pierre Loti, which portrayed life in Japan as highly exotic and refined. He preferred to think of the distant land in his own terms, as a place where artists lived in simple, but ideal conditions. Vincent imagined that the qualities he sought in his own working life—economy, simplicity, and harmony with nature—were in accord with life in Japan. He wrote to his brother that he planned to model his own life on that of a Japanese painter's, "living close to nature like a petty tradesman," hoping to one day "be something like old Tanguy" (Letter 540).

In the light and warmth of his first Provençal summer Vincent felt a heightened sensitivity. He experienced an unprecedented awareness of his surroundings, explaining to his brother that in Arles "you see things with an eye more Japanese, you feel color differently." He cultivated speed in his work, for he believed that "the Japanese draw

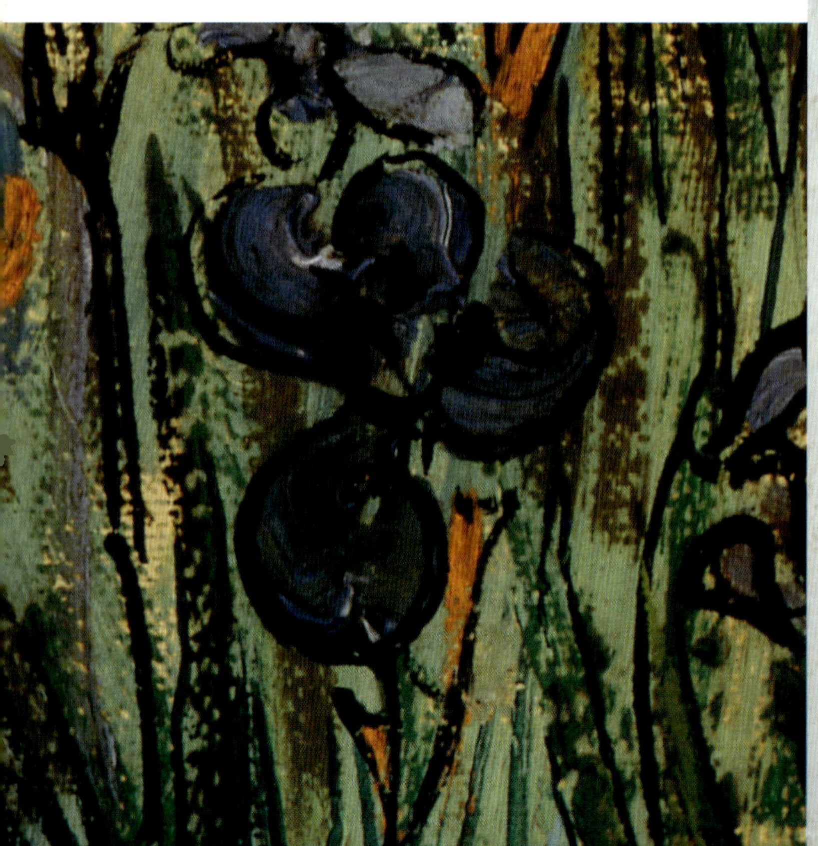

"A little town surrounded by fields all covered with yellow and purple flowers; exactly—can't you see it?—like a Japanese dream."

Letter to Theo, May 1888

Field with Flowers near Arles RIGHT AND LEFT MAY 1888. VAN GOGH MUSEUM, AMSTERDAM

Summer in Arles began with a blaze of color as the wild irises bloomed in the green meadows. *Field with Flowers near Arles* shows the tones Vincent added to his palette in response to the new season: the pale yellow buttercups in the foreground, the grayish-green willows against the blue sky in the distance, and the deep blue irises, with their flamelike petals crowning tufts of bright green leaves. Vincent imagined that the fields of irises near Arles were as beautiful as any in Japan, "as far as limpidity of atmosphere and the gay color effects are concerned."

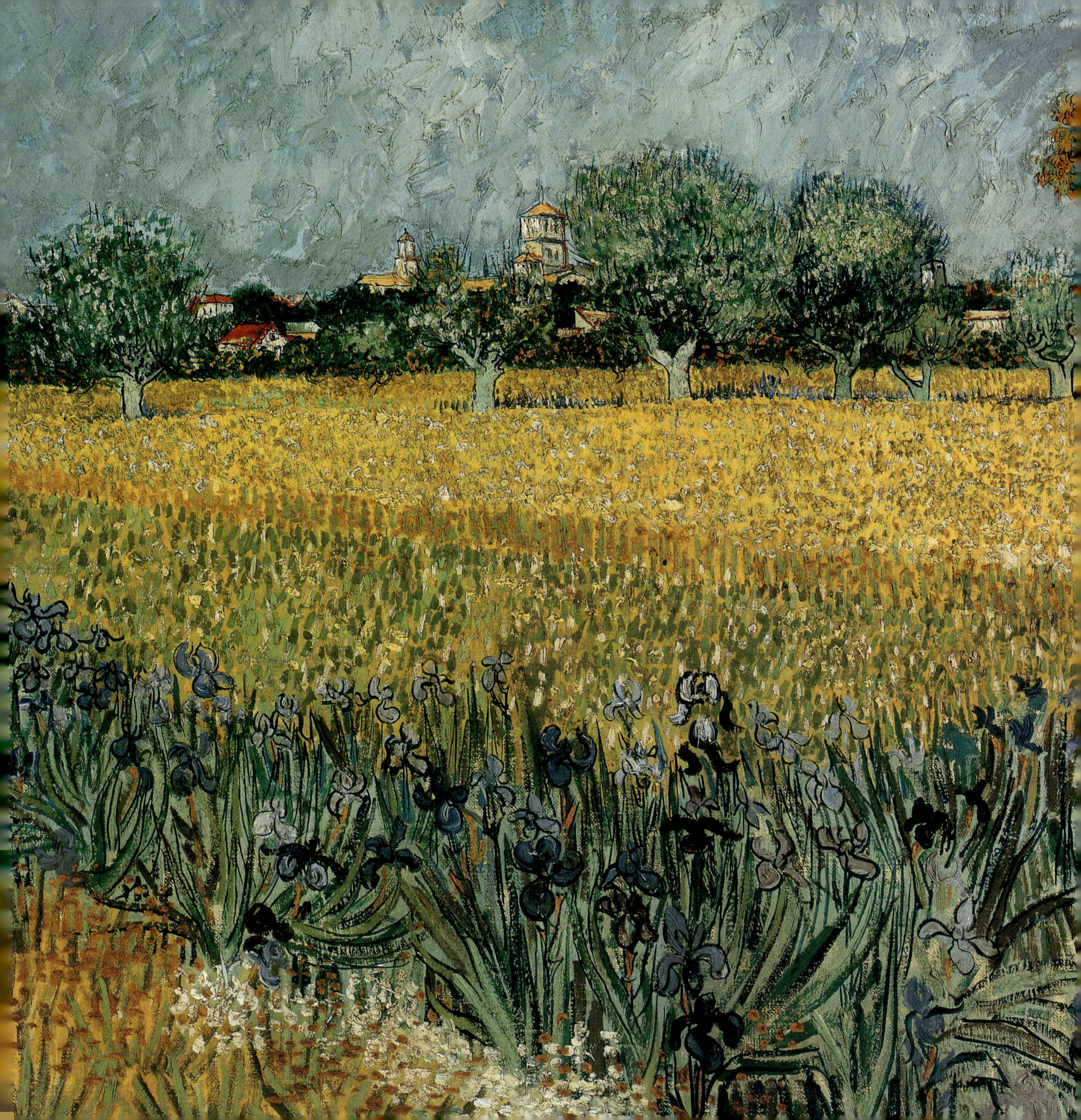

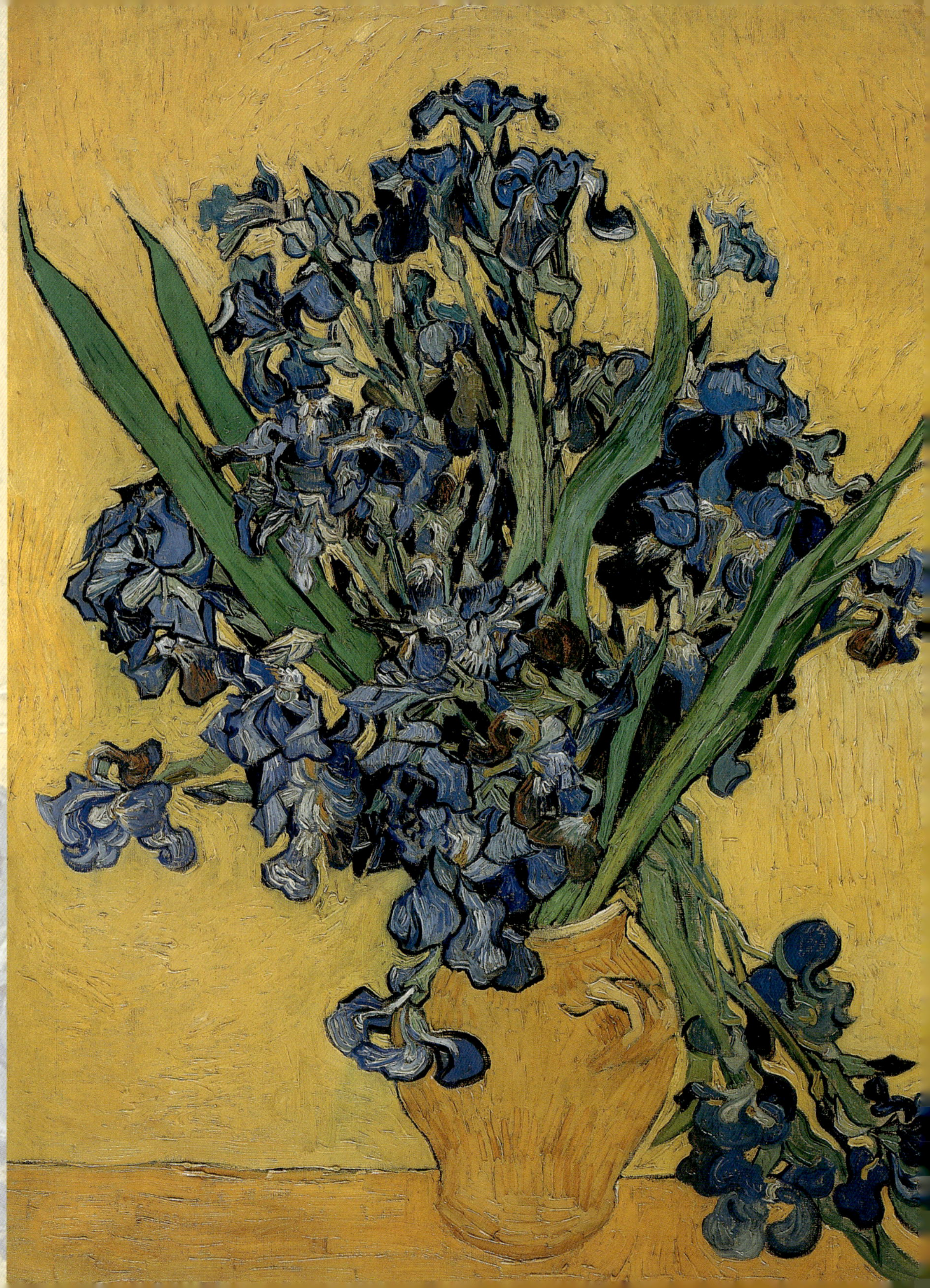

"It is good to love flowers, and ivy, and fir trees, and hawthorne hedges—they have been with us from the very beginning."

Letter to Theo, March 1877

quickly, very quickly, like a lightning flash, because their nerves are finer, their feeling simpler" (Letter 500). For Vincent, Japan served as a symbol of what he hoped to attain in his art and life.

In the green meadow, blooming with wild irises, Vincent pursued his ideal of Japan. He described it to Theo "like a Japanese dream," and he painted the scene quickly, knowing that the flowers would soon be mowed to make way for the cultivation of wheat. To depict the meadow, he drew upon his knowledge of Japanese composition. Clear bands of color, in tones of green and yellow, give *Field with Flowers near Arles* its unity of composition, while the subtle diagonal plane of the blooming irises, vivid in shades of blue, enliven the foreground.

Throughout the summer, Vincent continued to see Arles with a Japanese eye. The Langlois drawbridge reminded him of Hiroshige's print of *Sudden Shower on the Great Bridge*, and he depicted it as a pattern in yellow against a bright blue sky, with women quietly working on the riverbank, absorbed in the task of washing clothes. He favored a palette based on yellows and blues, using them to evoke vitality, whether he was painting a newly plowed meadow, a field of wheat, or a sidewalk café lit by gaslight. The blooming irises illustrated a natural lesson in color, convincing him that "there are colors which cause each other to shine brilliantly, which form a *couple*, which complete each other like a man and woman."

In the early summer of 1889, during his first weeks in residence at the Saint-Rémy asylum, Vincent longed to take his easel and paints into a meadow to paint the colorful flowers. But, as a new patient, his doctors confined him to the hospital for observation. He lamented to Theo that by the time he was permitted to leave the grounds, the first blooms of the season would be gone: "For the flowers are short-lived and will be replaced by the yellow wheatfield"

Irises

MAY 1890. VAN GOGH MUSEUM, AMSTERDAM

Vincent spent his last weeks in Saint-Rémy painting bouquets. He looked forward to his move to Auvers, and in returning to his favorite subject he found an apt expression for his cautious optimism. This bouquet of blue irises in an ocher vase against a bright yellow background records his enduring consideration of what he called "the color question." The vibrancy of the image stems from its powerful contrast of primary colors—yellow and blue—tempered with green. Although painted indoors and arranged for effect, *Irises* affirms Vincent's belief that all true color theory was based on nature.

(Letter 593). But, from his room on the second floor in the rambling building of the former monastery, he could see the overgrown hospital garden, where bright blue irises pushed up above the tangle of weeds and grass.

Theo arranged for Vincent to use a first-floor room as a studio, and there he painted two images of irises, tall with elegant stalks topped by flaglike blossoms, an echo of the beauty he had found under the Provençal sun. For Vincent, the iris still embodied the hopes that led him to Arles, a poignant symbol of a better life, inspired by a vision of Japan, where the people "live in nature as though they themselves were flowers" (Letter 542).

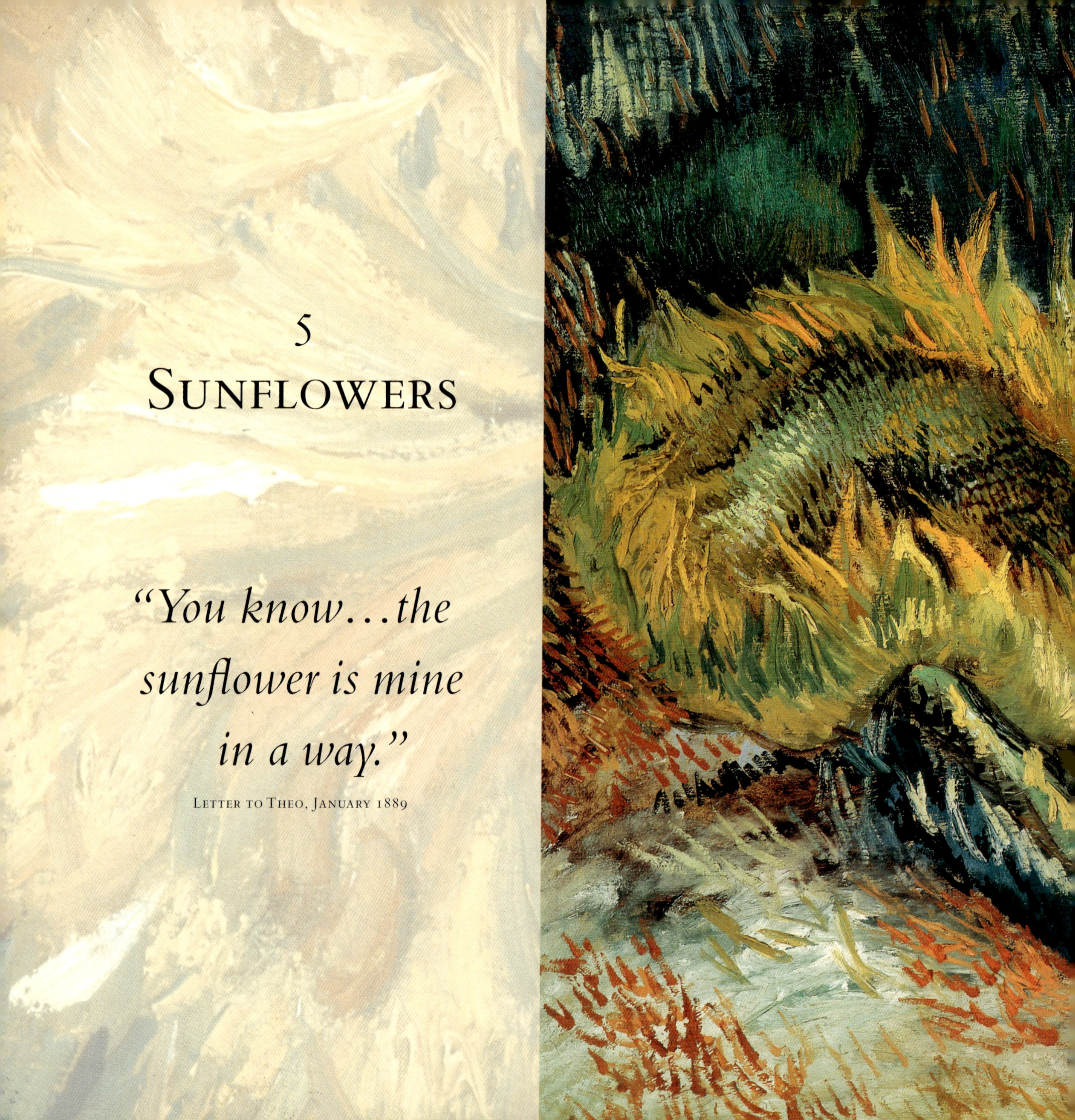

5
SUNFLOWERS

"You know…the sunflower is mine in a way."

Letter to Theo, January 1889

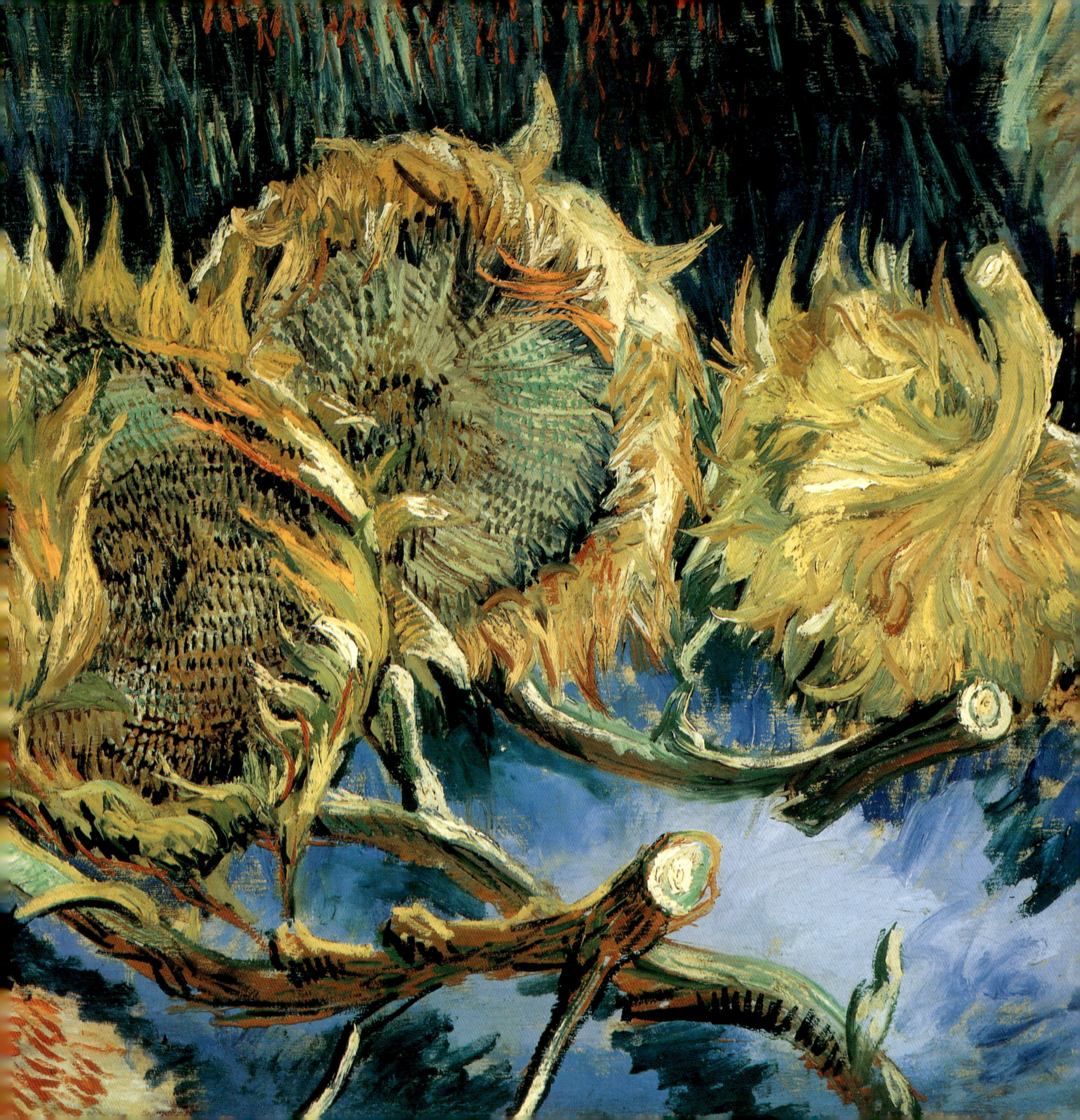

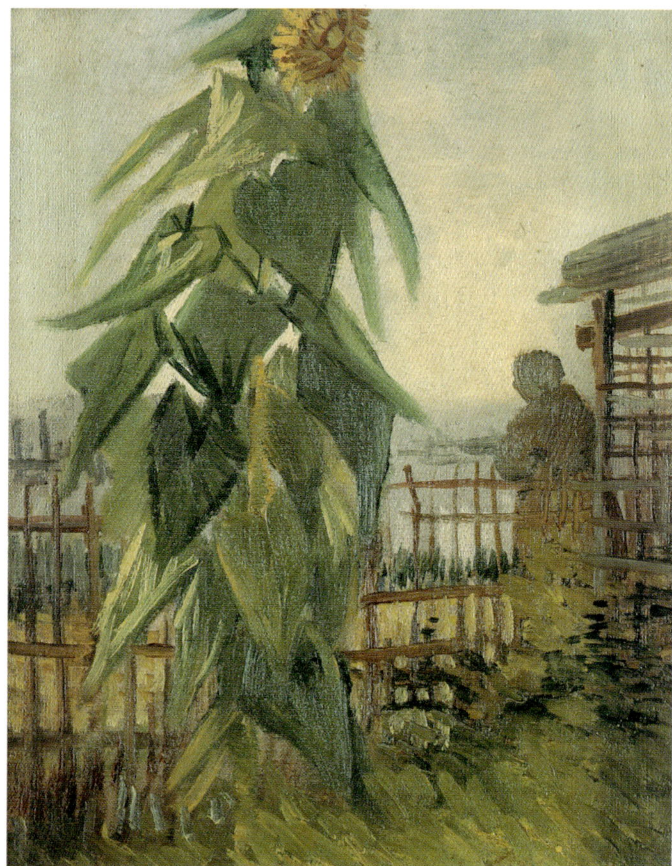

As Vincent worked on his own in Provence, loneliness blunted the pleasure of his new-found inspiration. At first he attributed his isolation to his total absorption in his art, explaining to Theo, "If I am alone—I can't help it, but honestly I have less need of company than of furiously hard work…It's the only time I feel I am alive, when I am drudging away at my work" (Letter 504). But early in July he sadly reported, "Often whole days pass without my speaking to anyone, except to ask for dinner or coffee. And it has been like that from the beginning" (Letter 508). Dressed in paint-spattered clothes and loaded down with his easel and paints, Vincent struck the townspeople of Arles as odd and even suspicious as he made his daily trek to the fields from his rented room over a café. Always awkward in social situations, and often in a state of excited enthusiasm, Vincent made few friends.

During his first months in the south, he met several other artists—Christian Mourier-Petersen from Denmark, the American Dodge MacKnight, and the Belgian painter Eugène Boch—but none of them had plans to remain in Arles. He struck up a relationship with a postal worker named Joseph Roulin, a solid, but liberal-minded citizen who reminded Vincent of Père Tanguy. Roulin proved to be a loyal friend, welcoming Vincent into his home and allowing him to paint portraits of him and his family, but Vincent wanted more than sympathetic companionship. He had hoped to find kindred souls, as passionate as he was in their commitment to the arts, but in this Arles failed to meet his expectations. He wrote to his brother explaining his situation, "When I came here I hoped it would be possible to make some connection with art lovers here, but up to the present I haven't made the least progress in people's affection" (Letter 508).

Lacking a circle of like-minded companions in Arles, Vincent expressed the hope that he could start an artists' community, believing that the high colors of the hot summer made Provence an ideal destination for painters. He enlisted Theo in his efforts to persuade other artists to join him and explained that the idea also made economic sense: a community of artists living together could share materials and household expenses and Theo's money would go further. In the company of other artists, Vincent would benefit from mutual criticism and encouragement; if his work improved it would—he had no doubt—start to sell. To bring his vision of the "Studio of the South" into being, Vincent invited the friends he had made in Paris to join him. Describing his dream to Theo, he confessed, "I wish everybody would come south like me" (Letter 492).

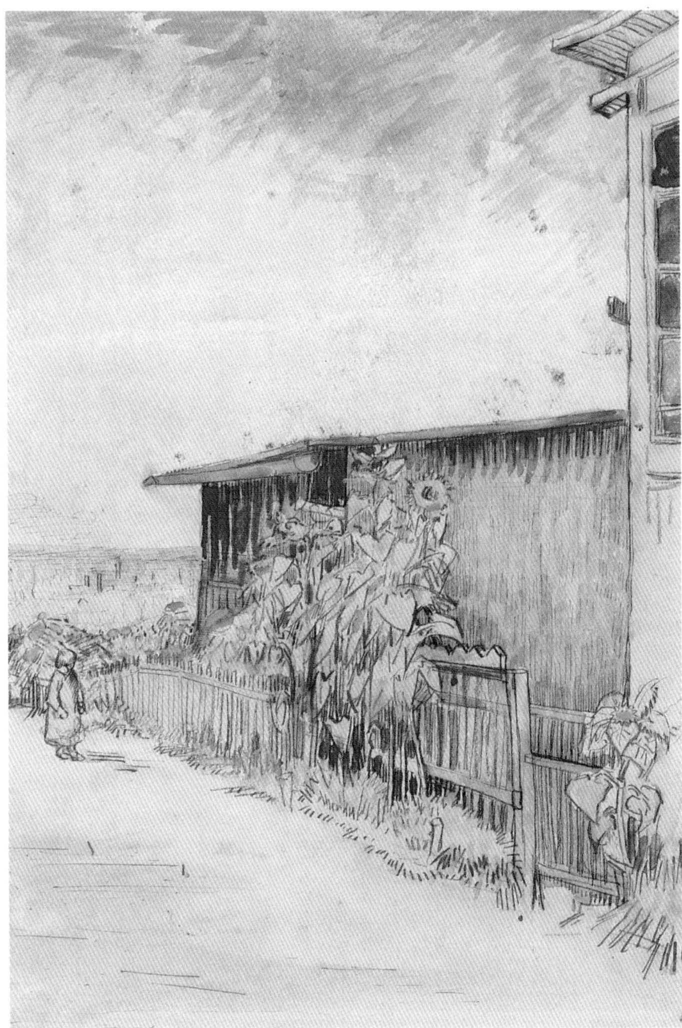

Allotment with Sunflowers on Montmartre FAR LEFT
SUMMER 1887. VAN GOGH MUSEUM, AMSTERDAM

During the summer months in Paris, Vincent regularly took his easel
to the semi-rural district on the outskirts of Montmartre. Typically,
he chose to paint a broad vista from a high point of view, featuring
the cultivated fields on the rolling hills and the quaint forms of
windmills against the bleached summer sky. In 1887 he painted
several studies of cottage gardens, with giant sunflowers towering
above the fences. Here the sunflower, with its broad orange bloom
nodding high upon its stalk, expresses a simple, rustic vitality in the
way it dominates the garden.

Shelter on Montmartre, with Sunflowers LEFT
SUMMER 1887. VAN GOGH MUSEUM, AMSTERDAM

Vincent quickly sketched this tall stand of sunflowers growing
against a simple wooden fence in pencil and ink, heightening it with
watercolor. In the summer of 1887 the sunflower had yet to acquire
a personal significance for Vincent. He enjoyed painting it as part of
the rural life that existed outside the center of the city, a life that he
regarded as more natural and picturesque than that of urban Paris.

Sunflowers PRECEDING PAGES
AUGUST–SEPTEMBER 1887. KRÖLLER-MÜLLER MUSEUM, OTTERLO

Vincent rarely included sunflowers in the bouquets he painted in
Paris, but late in the summer of 1887, he used the cut heads of several
blooms as subjects for still lifes. The desire to study color seems to
have inspired these works. In *Sunflowers*, Vincent varied the yellows
from pale citron to deep ocher, with the stems, centers, and brighter
grasslike strokes in the background making a vibrant contrast. He
painted the ragged petals and the twisted stems with a vigorous
impasto, suggesting the robust quality of the flower.

In a first step toward making his dream a reality, Vincent
rented four rooms in a house on the Place Lamartine in
Arles. He lacked the funds to furnish the rooms for living
and at first used them only as a studio and for storage. But
in July, Uncle Cent died, naming Theo as his main heir.
With typical generosity, Theo shared his windfall with his
brother, who used the money to transform the rough rooms
into an inviting residence. The building already had a
bright yellow exterior and whitewashed interior walls. To

"Under the blue sky the orange, yellow, red splashes of flowers take on an amazing brilliance, and in the limpid air there is a something or other happier, more lovely than in the North."

LETTER TO THEO,
AUGUST 1888

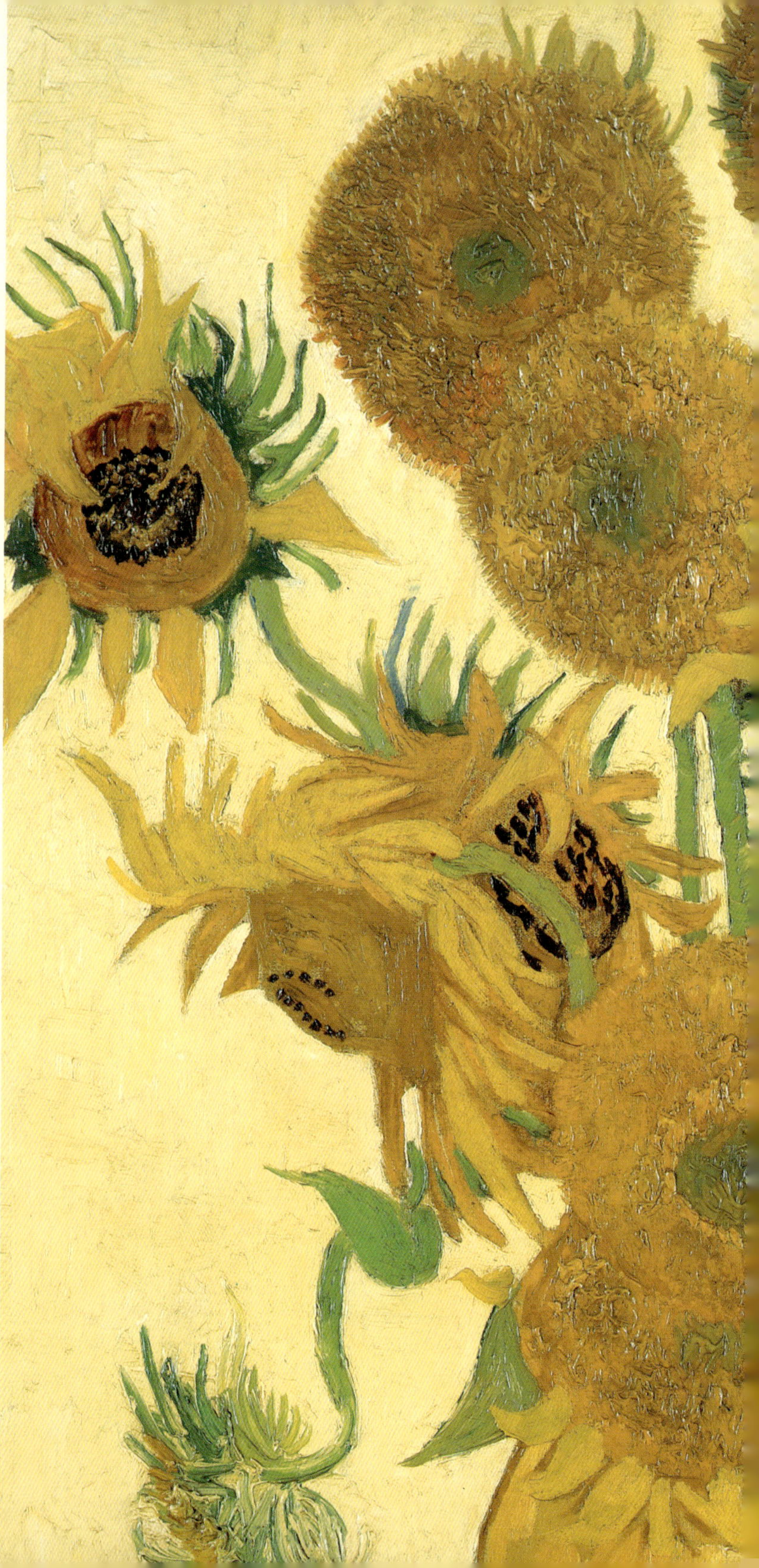

Still Life: Vase with Fourteen Sunflowers
AUGUST 1888. NATIONAL GALLERY, LONDON

Vincent began his series of sunflower paintings to enliven the studio of his Yellow House, but from the beginning they always meant more to him than simple decoration. Vincent hoped that his sunflower series would prompt discussions with his guests about art and illuminate for them the aesthetic experience of painting in the south. He believed that *Still Life: Vase with Fourteen Sunflowers* was the best of his series, and he described it in a letter to his sister as "a picture all in yellow." Aside from a few touches of green in the stems and the blue contour lines of the vase and table, Vincent restricted his palette to a subtle range of yellows, from the palest sun-struck tone to the ruddiest ocher.

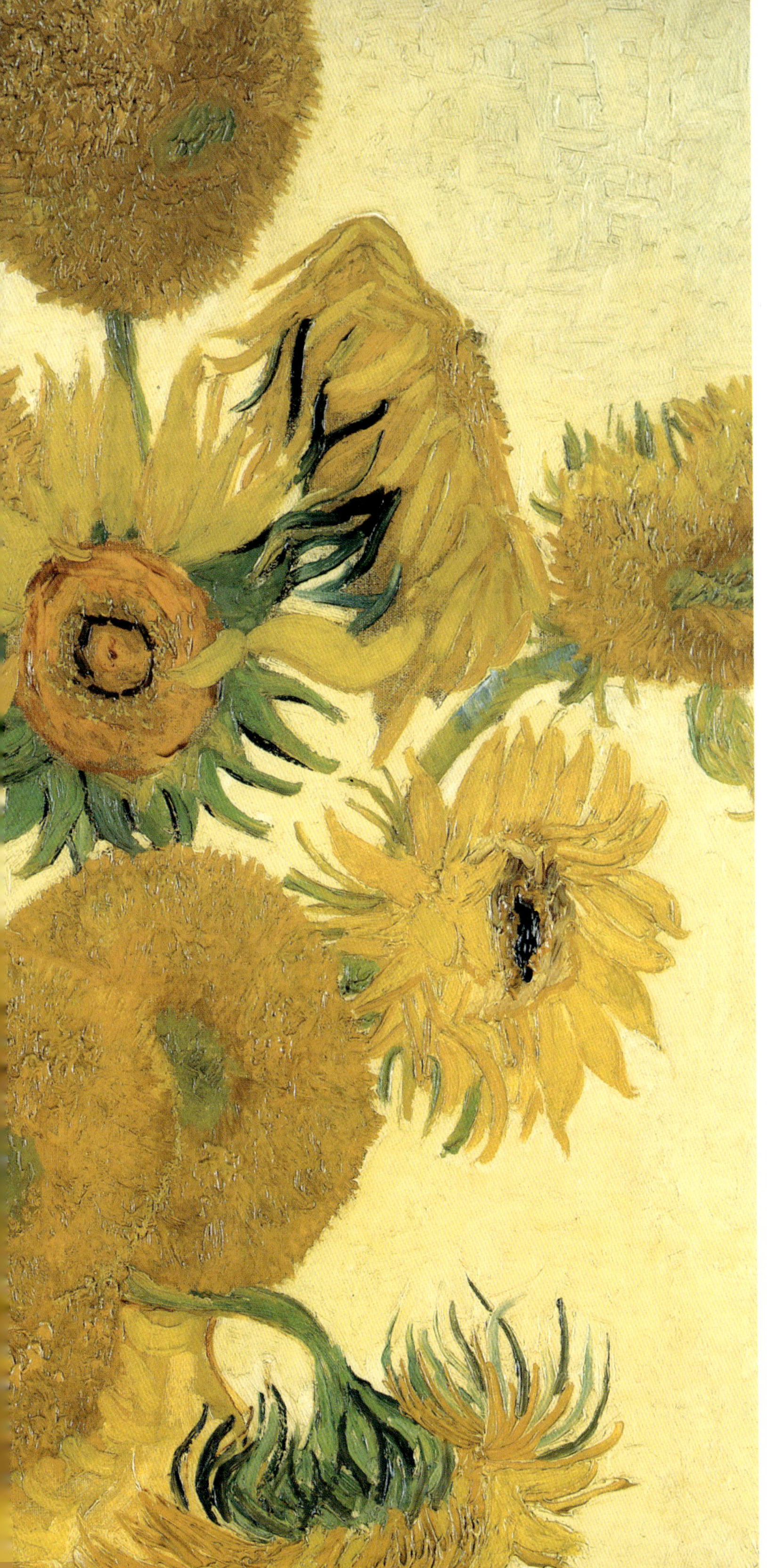

embellish the plain rooms, Vincent began to paint bouquets of sunflowers as visual gifts for the guests who would come to stay at the Yellow House. He wrote to his brother how he longed to share his passion for summer in Provence: "I keep wishing for the day when you will see and feel the sun of the South!" (Letter 522).

Vincent first painted sunflowers during his last summer in Paris and on a few occasions had combined them with other flowers, such as roses, in his paintings of bouquets. They also appear in his *plein-air* studies of the little farms of Montmartre. Vincent particularly liked the giant sunflowers he saw in those plain cottage gardens. Rising on thick, leafy stalks, the broad blooms towered above fences, sheds, and even barns. The ragged yellow petals, surrounding heads dense with brown seeds, provided a bright spot of color against the pale glare of a summer sky. For Vincent, the sunflower had yet to acquire a more personal meaning; in these early works, it made an appealing subject with its strong color and form, suggesting, perhaps, a simple vigor in contrast to more cultivated blooms.

Sunflowers were also a feature of cottage gardens in Arles. Vincent used a reed pen to sketch a patch of them in midsummer, but it was his attachment to the color yellow, rather than the rustic gardens, that gave the sunflower a particular significance for him. For Vincent, yellow was summer's hue, expressing the health-giving heat of the southern sun. He described the beauty of the Provençal summer to Theo, believing that the experience made an indelible impression on his perceptions: "Just now we are having a glorious strong heat, with no wind, just yellow, pale sulfur yellow, pale golden citron. How lovely yellow is! And how much better I shall see the North!" (Letter 522).

In mid-August, he wrote to Bernard about working in the unrelenting heat. "It beats down on one's head," he confessed. "I haven't the slightest doubt that it makes one

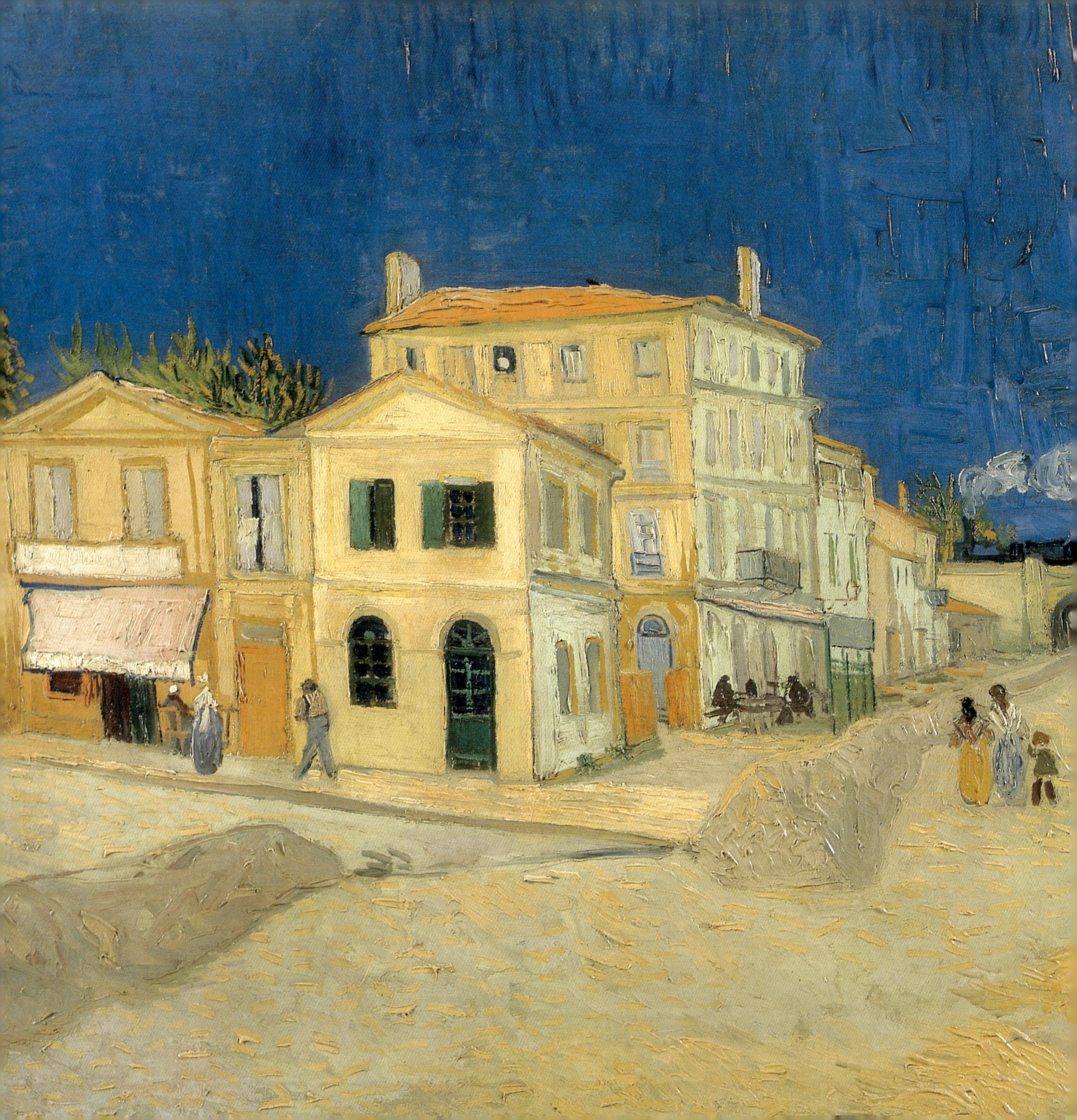

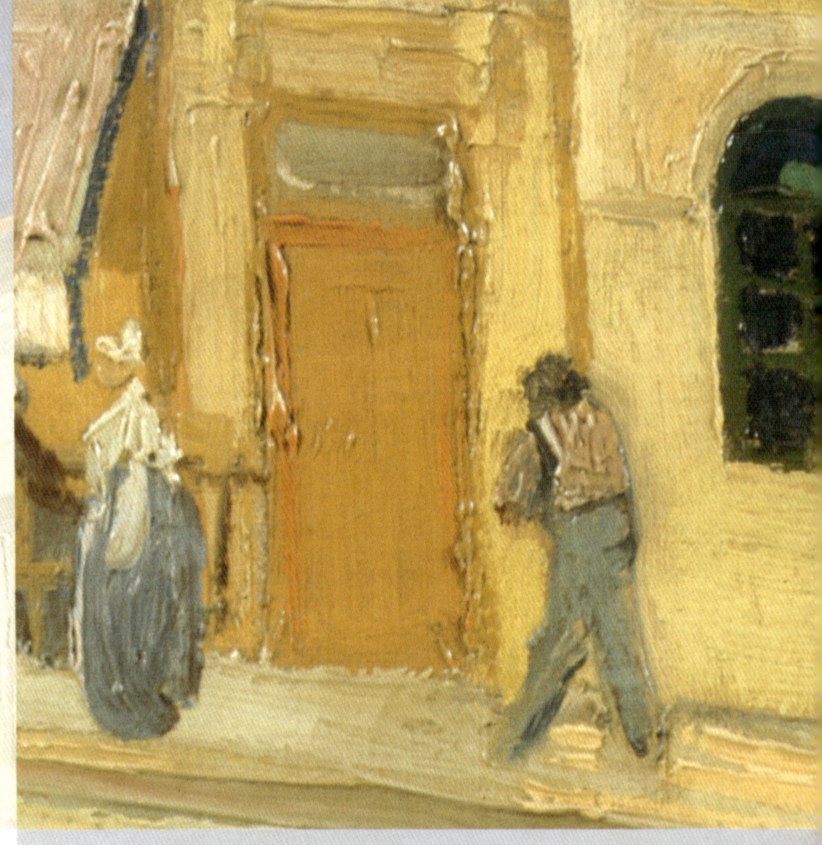

The Yellow House LEFT AND ABOVE
SEPTEMBER 1888. VAN GOGH MUSEUM, AMSTERDAM

crazy. But as I was so to begin with, I only enjoy it." In this same letter, Vincent told Bernard of his plan to brighten the walls of his Yellow House with pictures: "I am thinking of decorating my studio with half a dozen pictures of 'sunflowers,' a decoration in which the raw or broken chrome yellows will blaze forth on various backgrounds— blue, from the palest malachite green to *royal* blue, framed in thin strips of wood painted with orange lead." Vincent's meticulous description of color combinations suggest his investigation into the natural qualities of complementary and contrasting tones was continuing. His vivid language also reveals that paintings of sunflowers would bring the vital force of the sun indoors, warming his studio long after summer had ended.

Late in May, at the same time that Vincent first rented the Yellow House, Paul Gauguin wrote to Theo from Pont-Aven asking for financial help. For the past two months he

On September 8, Vincent wrote to Wil, "My house here is painted the yellow color of fresh butter on the outside with glaringly green shutters; it stands in the full sunlight in a square… And over it there is an intensely blue sky." Although he had rented the rooms in May, financial constraints prevented him from furnishing them as a residence until later that summer. He planned to use the two rooms on the upper floor as bedrooms. In his own, he placed a simple bed, an unpainted table, and rush-bottomed chairs. For the other room he planned elegant appointments, including a walnut bedstead, a matching night stand, and a blue coverlet. The walls were to be covered with bright paintings of sunflowers. With such a beautifully furnished room, Vincent happily told his sister, "I shall always be able to receive somebody as a guest."

had been unable to pay his creditors, and he now feared that without some remuneration they would press legal action. Hearing the news, Vincent offered a solution: send Gauguin a train ticket and persuade him to move to Arles. They could live together, sharing expenses, which would ultimately benefit Theo for, as Vincent pointed out, "You can't send him what will keep him going in Brittany and me what keeps me going in Provence." Vincent believed they could both live comfortably on his regular allowance and, if Gauguin agreed to send Theo a painting every month, Theo would actually make a profit. Gauguin's presence would also relieve Vincent's intense loneliness:

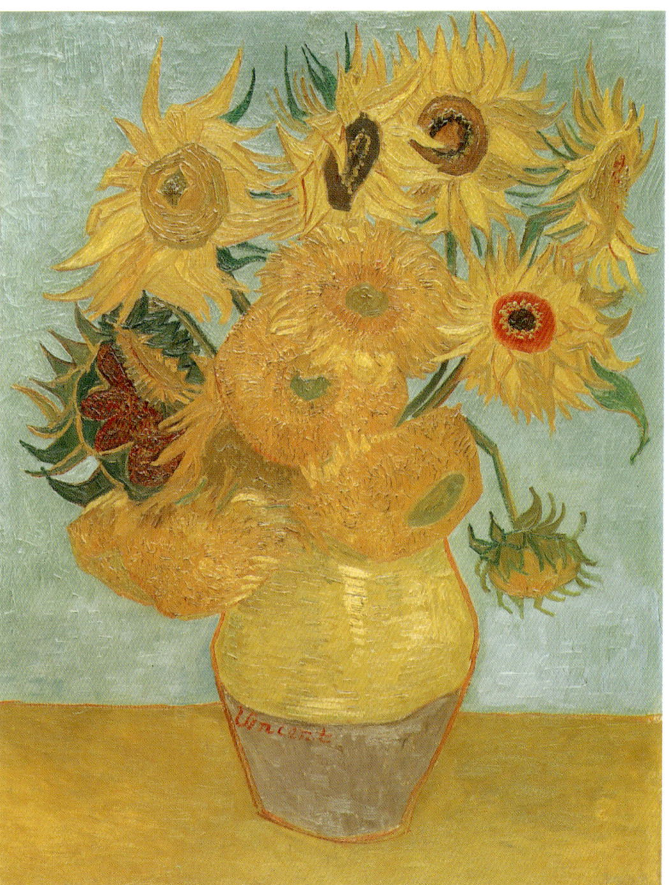

"You know that I have always thought it idiotic the way painters live alone. You always lose by being isolated… Besides it has always been my idea to join hands with other people" (Letter 493).

Vincent drafted a letter of invitation to Gauguin early in June. He told his friend that he had recently rented four rooms and he was seeking the company of "another painter inclined to work in the South, and who, like myself, would be sufficiently absorbed in his work to be able to resign himself to living like a monk who goes to the brothel once a fortnight." Vincent discussed the advantage of sharing expenses, and he emphasized the stimulating environment of Provence, "where working out of doors is possible nearly all the year round." He also admitted that he was eager for company: "Being all alone, I am suffering a little under this isolation. So I have often thought of telling you so frankly." While Gauguin did not reject Vincent's invitation, he was slow to accept it, postponing his journey to Arles by pleading illness and other commitments. His ambivalence did not deter Vincent, however. By the end of the summer, he was fully absorbed in the task of preparing the Yellow House for Gauguin's arrival.

An artist's house

Vincent took great pleasure in his labors of transforming the rooms into what he described as "really an *artist's house*," filled with "pictures from top to bottom." The first-floor rooms were set up to serve as a studio and a kitchen, while the rooms upstairs were planned as bedrooms for himself and a guest. Vincent chose simple, sturdy furnishings for his own bedroom, but he lavished his attentions on the other room, which he believed was prettier and had a better view. He told Theo that he intended to decorate it "like the boudoir of a really artistic woman," and when he—or Gauguin—came to visit they would enjoy looking out on a public garden bathed in morning light. But the view within the room would also be spectacular: "You will see these great pictures of sunflowers, 12 or 14 to the bunch, crammed into this tiny boudoir with its pretty bed and everything else dainty." He assured his brother, "It will not be commonplace" (Letter 533).

Throughout the summer and into September Vincent painted bouquets of sunflowers in a state of enthusiasm he compared to that of a "Marseillais eating bouillabaisse" (Letter 526). He began work each day at sunrise, painting quickly to capture the vivid color and vigorous form of the blooms before they faded. By the middle of September, he

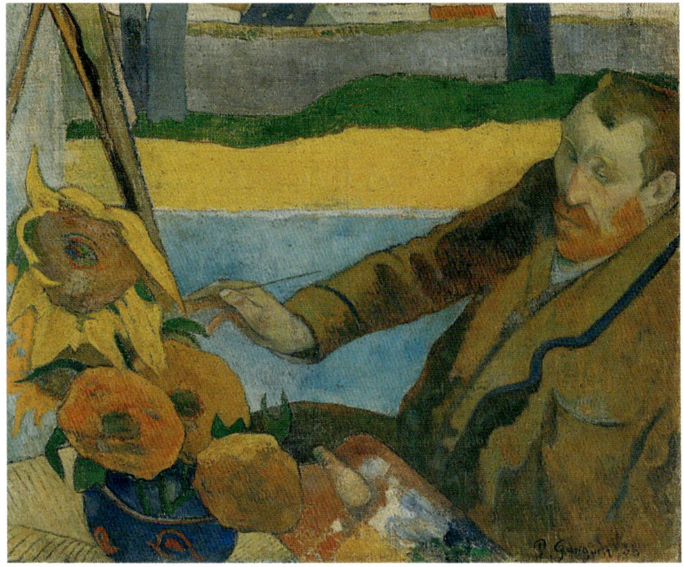

had moved into his Yellow House, but he was forced to abandon work on his series of sunflowers before he felt it was complete. Vincent wrote to his brother, "I wanted to do some more sunflowers too, but they were already gone" (Letter 543). He continued to wait for Gauguin's visit and early in October he wrote to him again, hoping to "hasten the possibility of your coming here." As Gauguin delayed further, Vincent's anxiety rose. His appetite diminished, and

Sunflowers FAR LEFT
JANUARY 1889. PHILADELPHIA MUSEUM OF ART

During the cold winter months, when sunflowers could not be obtained, Vincent used his own paintings as models, varying the colors of the vases and backgrounds. In 1890, in a letter to the art critic Albert Aurier, Vincent explained that his sunflowers expressed gratitude, perhaps for the failed attempt at companionship that briefly relieved him of his loneliness. But they also remained for him a source of strength, for even in the winter they radiated the warmth of the southern sun.

Portrait of Van Gogh Painting Sunflowers, **Paul Gauguin** LEFT
DECEMBER 1888. VAN GOGH MUSEUM, AMSTERDAM

Gauguin paid tribute to Vincent's passion for sunflowers in a portrait he painted early in December 1888. Much later, in October 1903, when recalling his stay in Arles, Gauguin claimed that the portrait startled Vincent, who looked at the work and said, "That's me all right, but me gone mad." The portrait honors the bond of friendship between the two artists, although they never saw each other again after Gauguin's departure from Arles.

he reported to Theo that he existed mainly on coffee and bread. By the time Gauguin finally arrived in Arles on October 23, Vincent was overwrought with anticipation.

Gauguin's visit

At first Gauguin's presence calmed Vincent. Gauguin took over the chore of cooking and encouraged him in his work. But he was a private and aloof man, hardly willing to be the constant companion that Vincent expected. Soon winter set in and both men found the small rooms of the Yellow House increasingly cramped and claustrophobic. Their discussions about art became debates, then hostile arguments. Vincent demanded more attention, which Gauguin answered with disdain. Life together proved impossible, and ultimately it ended in disaster.

But early in December, Gauguin painted a portrait of Vincent that revealed a sympathetic understanding for his troubled friend and his elusive dreams. He portrayed him at an easel, dabbing color on a canvas. And although it was winter, Vincent was painting sunflowers: a resplendent yellow bouquet in a cobalt-blue vase. By this time the relationship between the two men was irreparably frayed, but Gauguin respected Vincent's intense struggle for artistic vision. Vincent had feared that Gauguin would not fully comprehend the artistic advantage of Provence if he came too late in the year, writing to Bernard in anticipation of the visit, "the only thing to be regretted will be that it is winter and not the season for fine weather." Gauguin, however, easily identified the source of Vincent's passionate inspiration—and the depth of his painful yearning—when he saw the paintings of sunflowers. Years later Gauguin wrote: "In my yellow room, sunflowers with purple eyes stand out on a yellow background, they bathe their stems in a yellow pot on a yellow table...Oh yes! he loved yellow,

Twelve Sunflowers in a Vase RIGHT AND LEFT
SEPTEMBER 1888. NEUE PINAKOTHEK, MUNICH

In the fall of 1888, Vincent received word from Gauguin that he would at last come to Arles. Vincent's excitement propelled him into a state of urgent activity, preparing the Yellow House for its first guest. He wrote to Theo that his series of sunflowers for the studio was well under way, and that he was particularly pleased with an image of twelve flowers and buds in a yellow vase that employed a color scheme he described as "light on light." He used his paint lavishly, sculpting the petals with thick impasto and filling the background with basket-weave brush strokes in pale green and white. He told Theo he had to "do the whole in one rush" for sunflowers faded so soon.

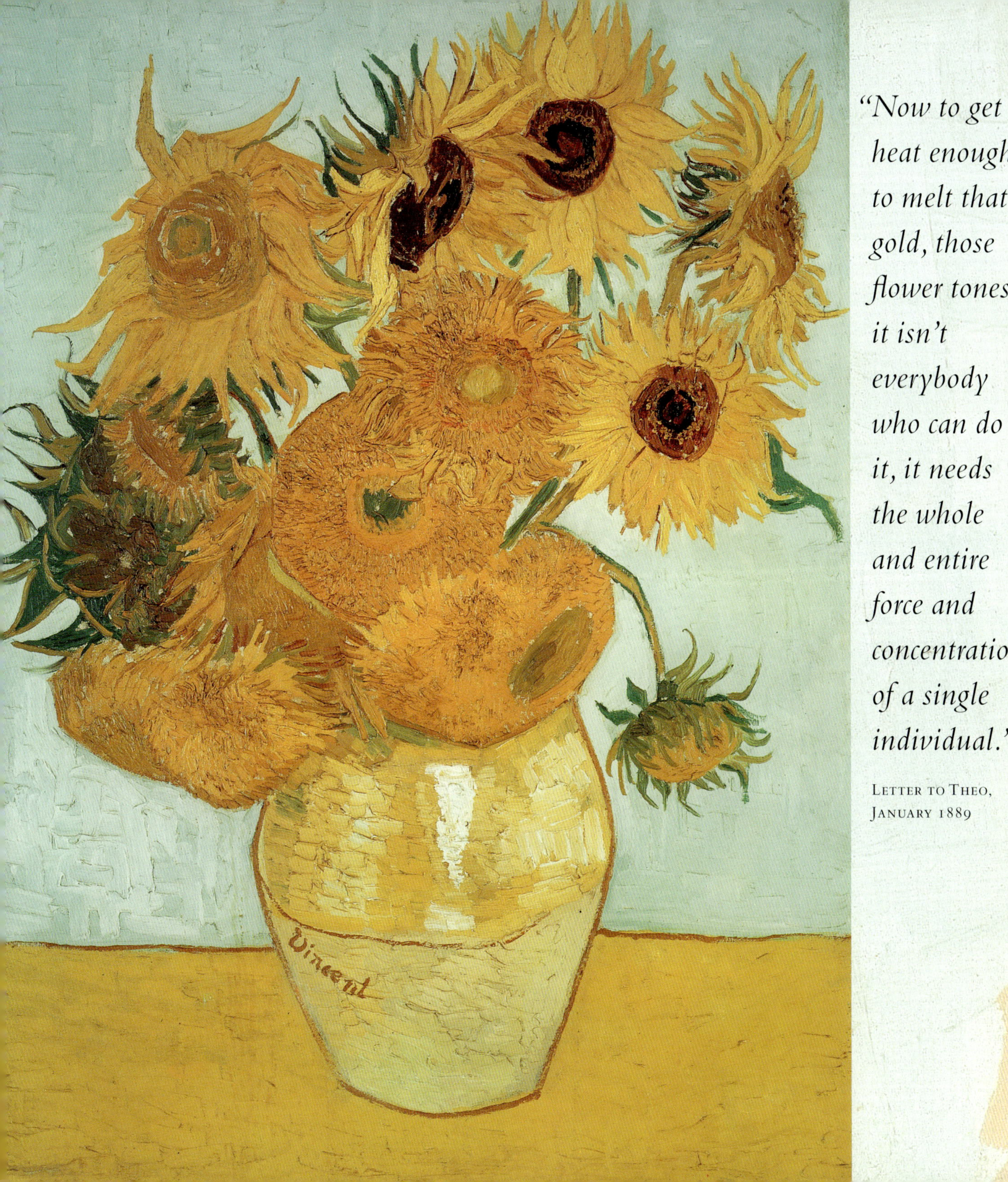

"*Now to get up heat enough to melt that gold, those flower tones, it isn't everybody who can do it, it needs the whole and entire force and concentration of a single individual.*"

LETTER TO THEO,
JANUARY 1889

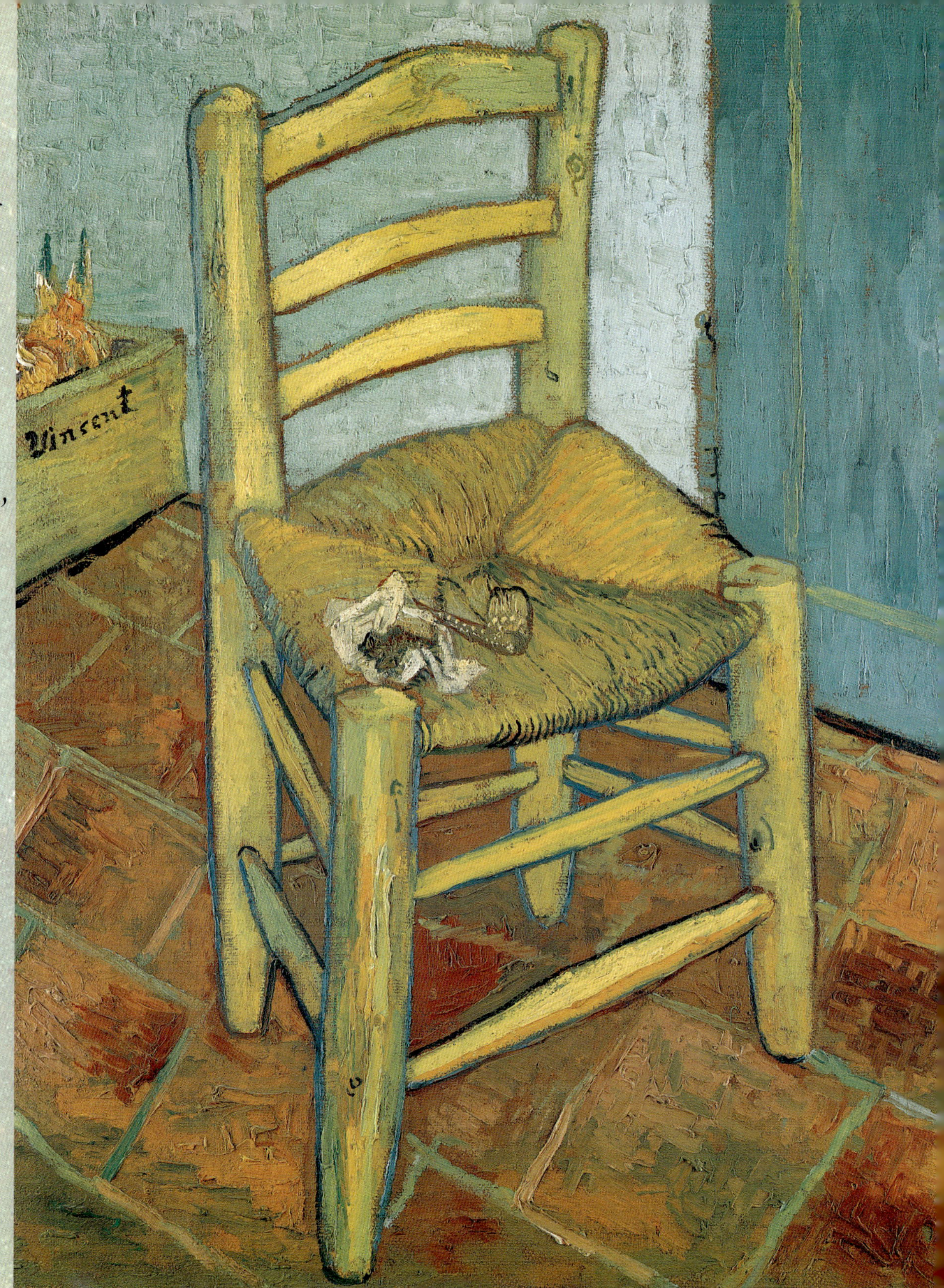

*"It does me a
tremendous
amount of
good to have
such intelligent
company as
Gauguin's,
and to see
him work."*

Letter to Theo,
December 1888

Vincent's Chair with his Pipe LEFT
NOVEMBER 1888. NATIONAL GALLERY, LONDON

Gauguin's Chair RIGHT
NOVEMBER 1888. VAN GOGH MUSEUM, AMSTERDAM

Vincent portrayed his life with Gauguin in Arles in these paintings of chairs. For Gauguin, he selected an armchair with an upholstered cushion; his own had simple unpainted wood and a rush seat. The objects on each chair evoke the spirit of an absent model. The pile of books and burning candle suggest Gauguin's intellectual complexity, while the pipe and pouch of tobacco signal Vincent's own modesty. Both works remained unfinished when Vincent entered the hospital in December. After his release in January 1889, he put the final touches on the portrait of his chair, signing his name on the box of sprouting bulbs in the background.

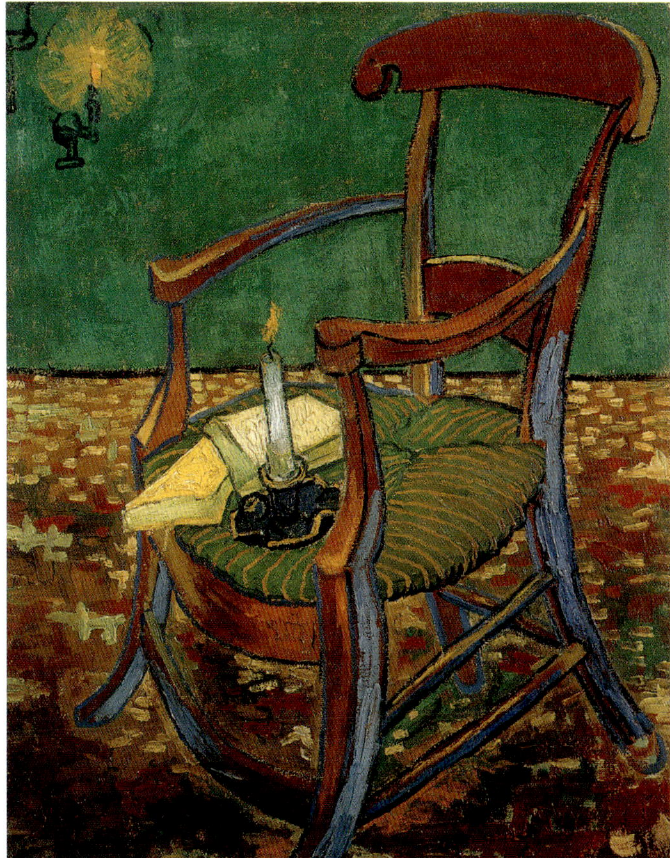

this good Vincent…those glimmers of sunlight rekindled his soul, that abhorred the fog, that needed the warmth."

On leaving the hospital in early January 1889 after the incident of his self-inflicted wound, Vincent returned to the Yellow House to try to make sense of his shattered life. In his letters to Theo, he repeatedly reflected upon his paintings of sunflowers, modestly asserting "the sunflower is mine in a way" (Letter 573). He took comfort in recalling that Gauguin admired them, and he suggested that "Gauguin would be glad to have one," telling Theo to send him one of the two in his possession. Vincent assured Theo that he could always paint them again; in fact, he painted three bouquets of sunflowers that winter, using his own paintings as models for the flowers that were out of season.

But the original works remained a source of strength for Vincent in his most fragile days. In the sunflower, he had forged an icon for the power that created his art. In one of his last letters to his sister Wil, written in February 1890 from Saint-Rémy, Vincent confided that he felt a need to apologize "for the fact that my pictures are after all almost a cry of anguish." But he noted a difference in his images of "the rustic sunflower" and he felt that they might be a symbol of gratitude. While painting the sunflowers, Vincent experienced a rare balance in his life, when his expressive power equaled his inspiration and his desire to live as part of a community of like-minded artists seemed—to him—at last to be at hand.

6
FIELDS

"It is not the language of painters but the language of nature which one should listen to."

LETTER TO THEO, JULY 1882

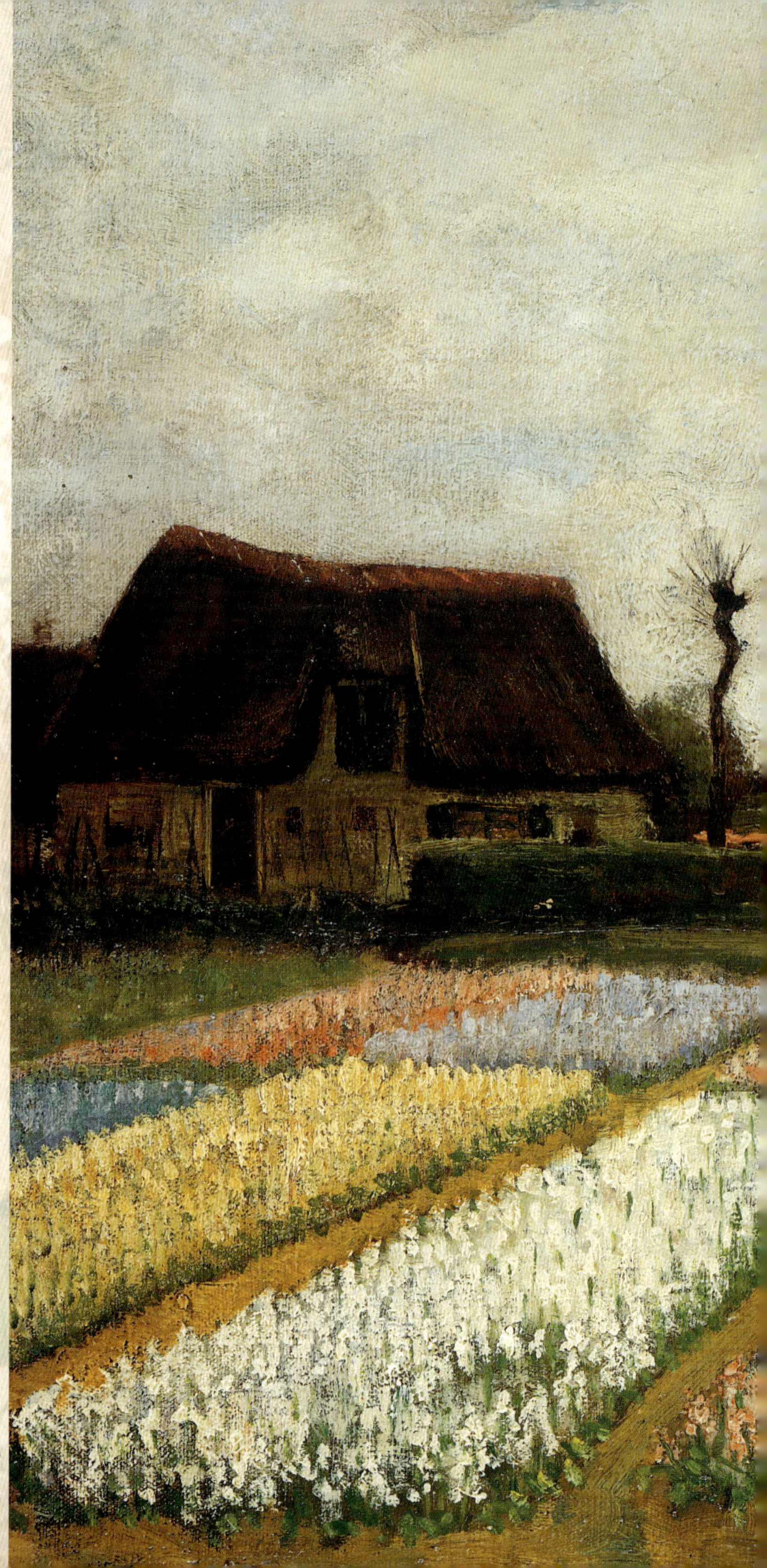

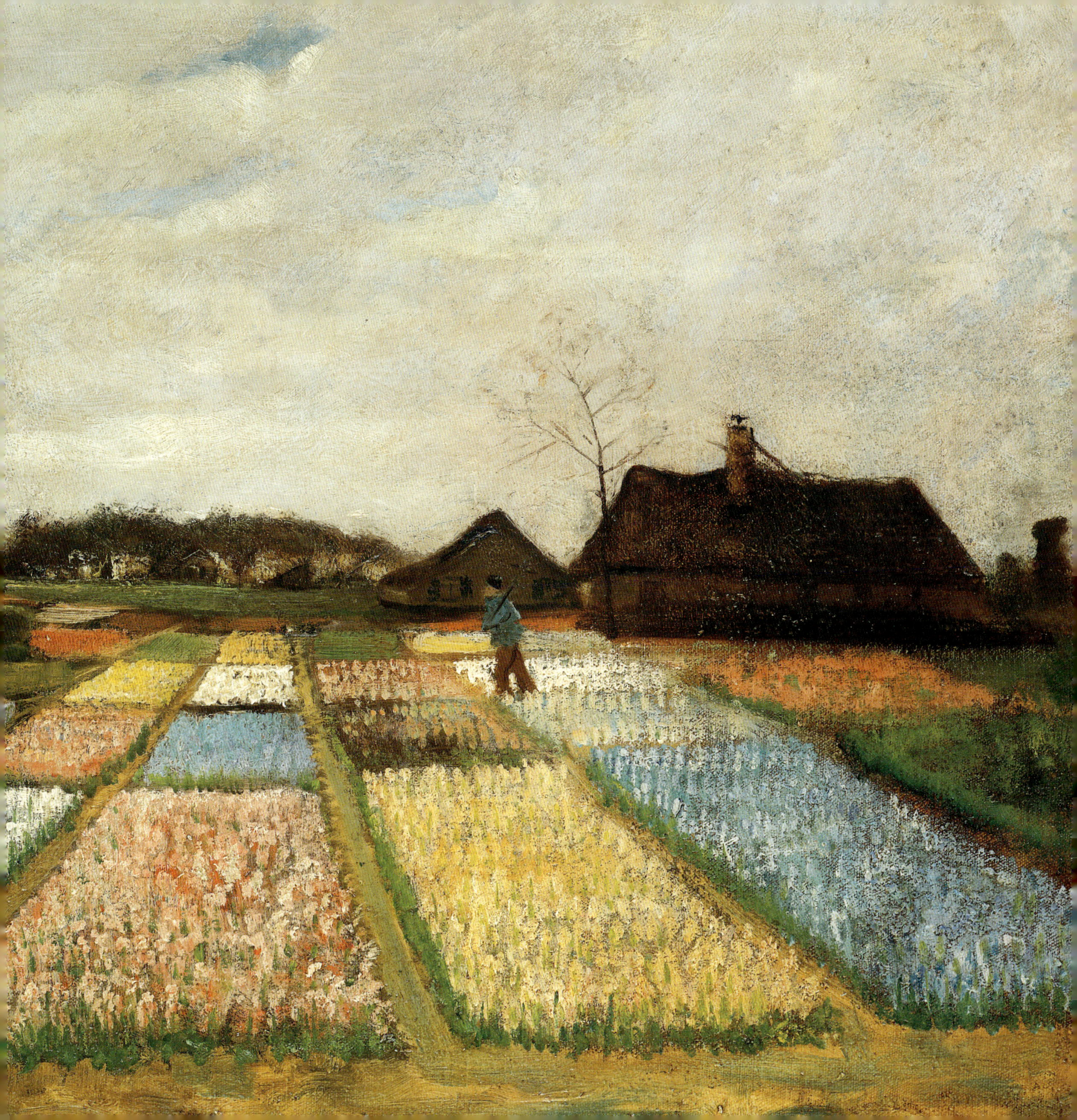

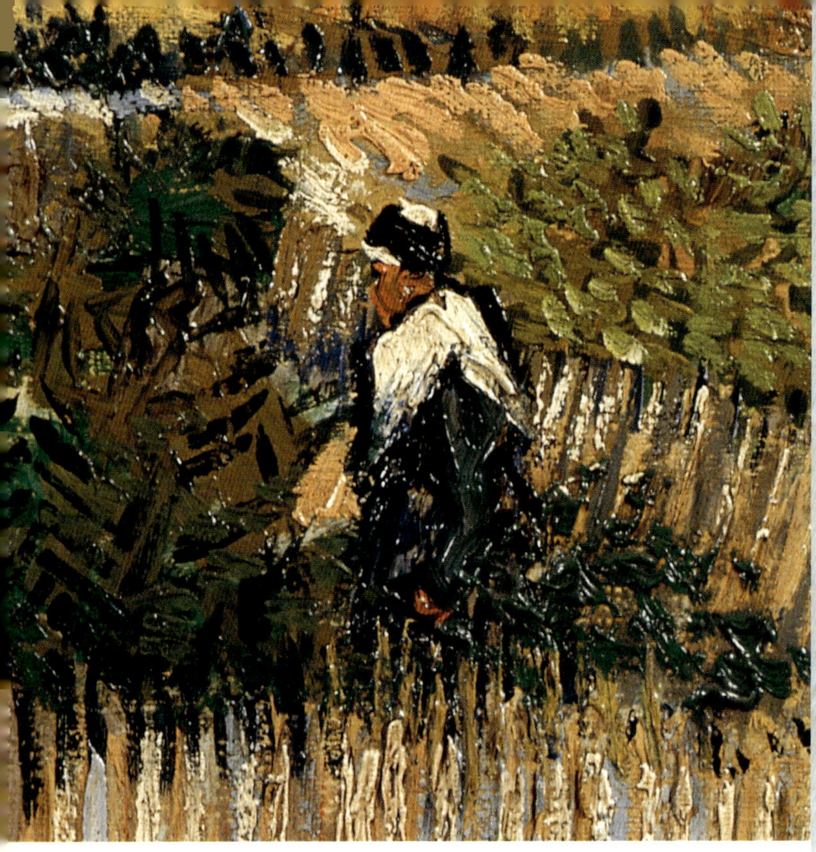

Vincent's last months in Arles were clouded by the specter of his illness. In January 1889, after a brief stay in the hospital where he was treated for delusions and for loss of blood from his self-inflicted wound, he returned to the Yellow House to convalesce. He was intent on resuming his work, believing that it would restore his health and stability, but his efforts proved futile. Burdened by shame and weakened by chronic insomnia, he lived in terror of another seizure.

In mid-February, Vincent suffered a second attack and stayed in the hospital for a week. But after his release, his neighbors, worried by his behavior, petitioned the mayor of Arles to have him either readmitted or returned to his family. Vincent was kept under medical supervision with privileges to receive guests. When his condition allowed, he was permitted to leave the hospital grounds to paint. Although the limitations of this life stifled him, Vincent feared that he was now unable to tolerate the stress of living

The Harvest RIGHT AND LEFT
JUNE 1888. VAN GOGH MUSEUM, AMSTERDAM

In *The Harvest*, Vincent hoped to attain something of the rural grandeur that Cézanne expressed in his harvest scenes painted in Provence. The rolling terrain, with its open vista and rugged hills in the distance, is depicted with the Provençal master's command of spatial organization. But Vincent also captured a strong sense of atmosphere, of the scorching sun beating down on the golden fields uninterrupted by shade or shadow.

Flower Beds in Holland PRECEDING PAGES
APRIL 1883, NATIONAL GALLERY OF ART, WASHINGTON D.C.

Vincent painted this small study of bulb fields in flower during his second year in The Hague. The light and luminous colors of the blooming fields mark the passing beauty of the spring season. His low point of view offers a panoramic vista, the bright plots seeming to rise to meet the low horizon. The darker, earth-toned forms of the thatched cottages, with bare-branched trees beside them, give the composition a firm basis.

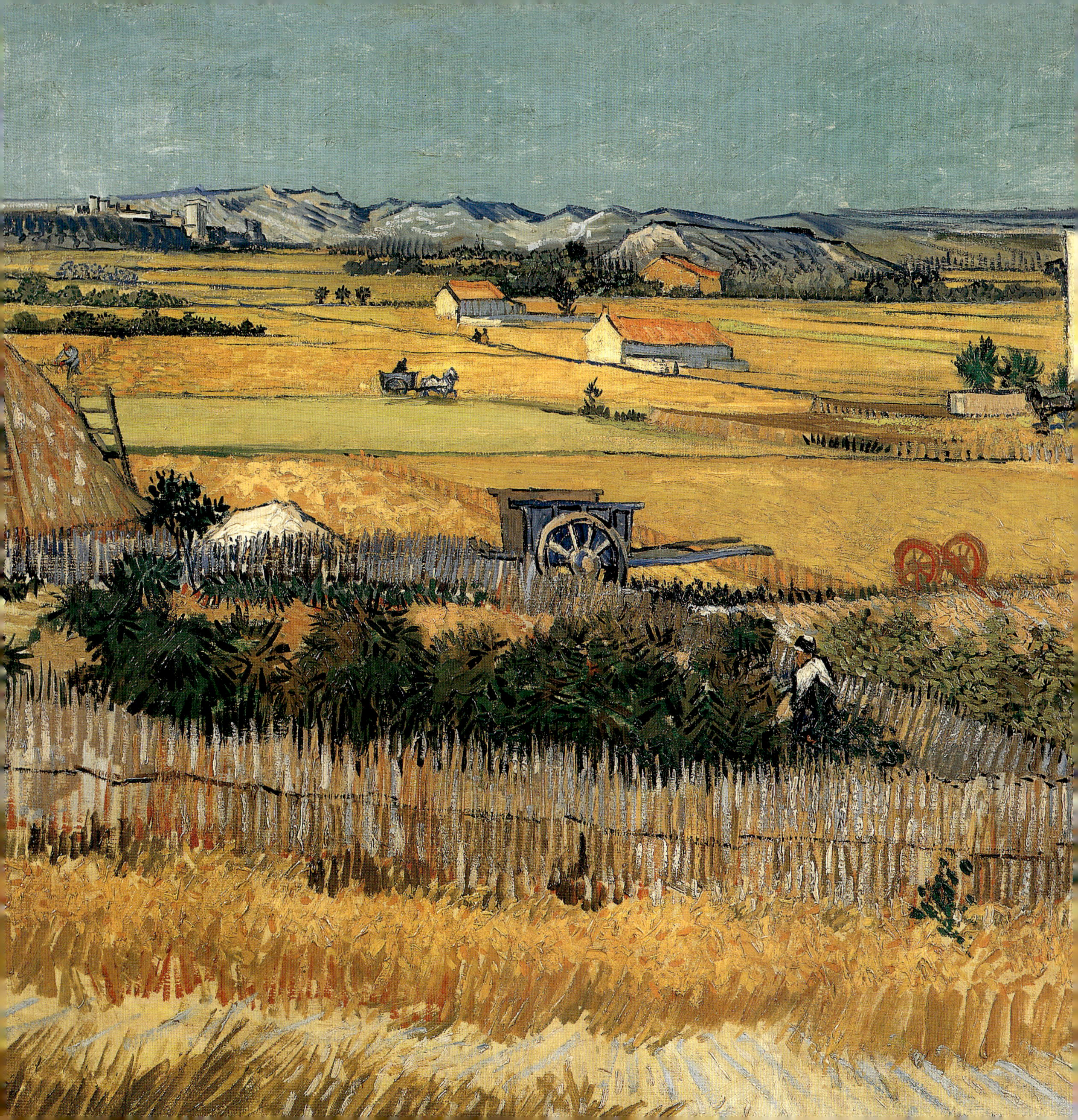

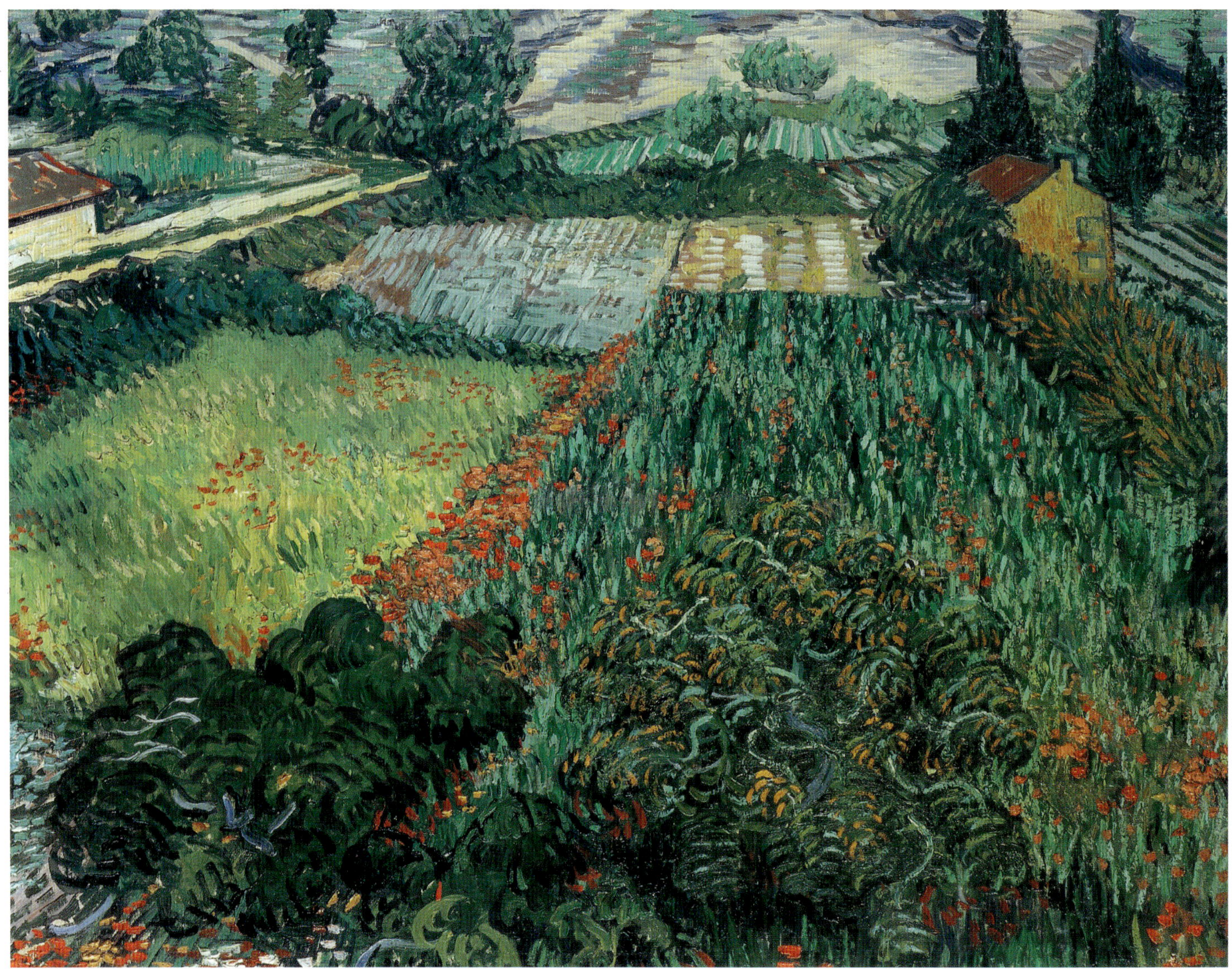

alone. In May, he voluntarily entered the mental asylum of Saint-Paul-de-Mausole, which was located fifteen miles from Arles in Saint-Rémy-de-Provence.

In the asylum Vincent at last found the secure refuge he sought. The presence of a sympathetic staff lessened his fear of future seizures, which he now accepted as inevitable, and his doctors readily understood his need to work. At first,

Vincent was required to remain indoors for observation, but he proved resourceful, selecting his subjects from the limited repertoire available in the gardens and grounds of the hospital. From his window, he could see the groves of olive and cypress trees, with the Alpilles hills rising beyond them. This was the view he painted in *The Starry Night*, but Vincent longed to venture out into the countryside to paint the fields that lay beyond the village of Saint-Rémy. Late in May, he could see the first grain crops under cultivation: "Through the iron-barred window I see an enclosed wheatfield…above which I see the morning sun rising in all its glory." Making the most of his limited view, Vincent made sketches of the distant hills, the groves of trees, and the changing crops. The thought that he might soon be able to take his easel out into the fields sustained him, and he wrote to Theo on June 9, "Face to face with nature it is the feeling for work that supports me" (Letter 594).

Rural inspirations

The cultivated field, tended patiently by the farm worker, endured in Vincent's artistic vision as a symbol of balance, an accord between humanity and the natural environment. His clear preference for rural subjects dates from his first years working for Goupil et Cie, when he discovered the Dutch naturalists of The Hague School and the French Barbizon painters. He was drawn to the paintings of Jean-François Millet, whose work brought an inherent dignity and a solemn melancholy to the basic routine of rural toil. Vincent collected prints of Millet's paintings, and in August 1880, shortly after he announced his intention to become a painter, he asked Theo to send him a set of reproductions of Millet's *Labors of the Field* to copy as part of his training. His acknowledgment of Millet's influence never wavered; in November 1889, he wrote to Theo from Saint-Rémy that "Millet has reawakened our thoughts so we can see the dweller in nature."

Like Millet, Vincent regarded rural labor as a timeless, universal endeavor, essential to existence. His ideas may have also been inspired by the traditional European iconography of the labors of the month, a symbolic division of the year according to the cycle of work on the land. During the Middle Ages, the scheme appeared in

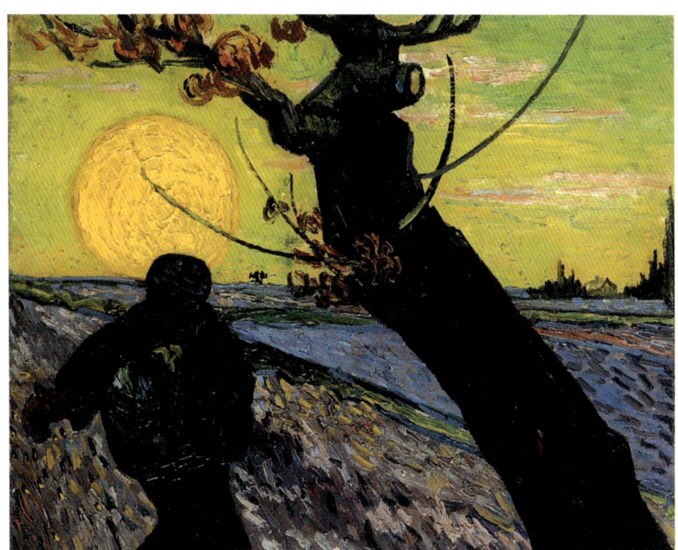

The Sower ABOVE
NOVEMBER 1888. VAN GOGH MUSEUM, AMSTERDAM

In *The Sower*, Vincent pays homage to Millet's lone farm laborer, using a Japanese-inspired composition and the hot palette of the blazing Provençal sun. He described the work to Theo as "a big field with clods of violet earth—climbing toward the horizon… a sower…Over it all a yellow sky with a yellow sun" (Letter 501). Vincent viewed the sower as a symbol of rural work, of the noble endeavor which sustains life.

Field with Poppies LEFT
JUNE 1889. KUNSTHALLE, BREMEN

During his first weeks in the asylum at Saint-Rémy, Vincent was confined to the hospital grounds. But by the middle of his second month, he was allowed to work in the fields under staff supervision. The high point of view of *Field with Poppies* may indicate that Vincent saw the scene from his second-story window, but the fresh color has the vitality of *plein-air* painting.

manuscript painting, in cathedral decoration, and as a terrestrial counterpart to the astrological calendar. Whatever his source, Vincent saw in the image of rural toil the unity of life and work. It became a subject that validated his endeavors as a painter, for more than any other it brought him "face to face with nature."

Vincent's deep attachment to rural life grew out of his early religious calling and his desire to aid the working poor. Land labor served to inspire his earliest endeavors in art. Rural locations marked the single chord of consistency during his restless years of struggle to secure his artistic identity, always leading him out of the city to seek solace in the country. While in Paris, Vincent preferred to set up his easel on the outskirts of the city and its suburbs, and he found the small farms of Montmartre and the rolling fields beyond Asnières a welcome relief from the artificiality of the urban environment.

When Vincent left Paris for Arles, he was seeking an antidote to the ills he attributed to city life. He wanted to work among the farmers and labor at his painting in the way they labored on the land, giving his art and life the value that he recognized in rural toil. The corn harvest in Provence in June 1888 satisfied his yearning. He painted in the fields in a state of exhilarated intensity, believing that the heat and the labor restored his health and spirits. He wrote with evident pride to Bernard, "I work even in the middle of the day, in the full sunshine, without any shadow at all, in the wheatfields, and I enjoy it like a cicada."

When painting *The Harvest*, Vincent recalled Cézanne's ability to render "the harsh side of Provence." Hard, bright yellows convey the scorching heat and the whole surface has an even tone; shadows are absent and there is not a cloud in the sky. The land rolls back to its low horizon with a simple, panoramic grandeur. Although this is cultivated

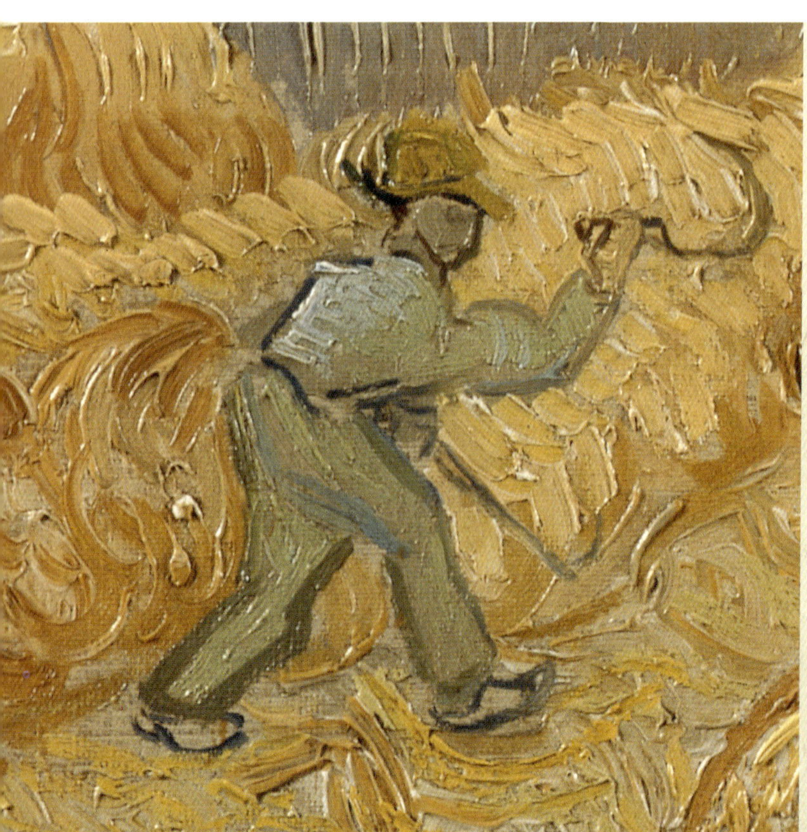

Wheatfield with a Reaper RIGHT AND LEFT
JULY–SEPTEMBER 1889. VAN GOGH MUSEUM, AMSTERDAM

Painted during his time at the Saint-Rémy asylum, *Wheatfield with a Reaper* reveals Vincent's enduring fascination with the labors of the field. Under a vibrant sun, the small anonymous figure makes his way through the swirling wheat, swinging his sickle and cutting the grain. Vincent claimed to have completed the painting during his first attack at Saint-Rémy, but in a letter to Theo, written in September after his recovery, he writes, "Reaper is finished…it is an image of death as the great book of nature speaks of it." In it Vincent sought to portray an aspect of benevolence, a death "almost smiling," and he confided to Theo, "I find it queer that I saw it like this from between the iron bars of a cell" (Letter 604).

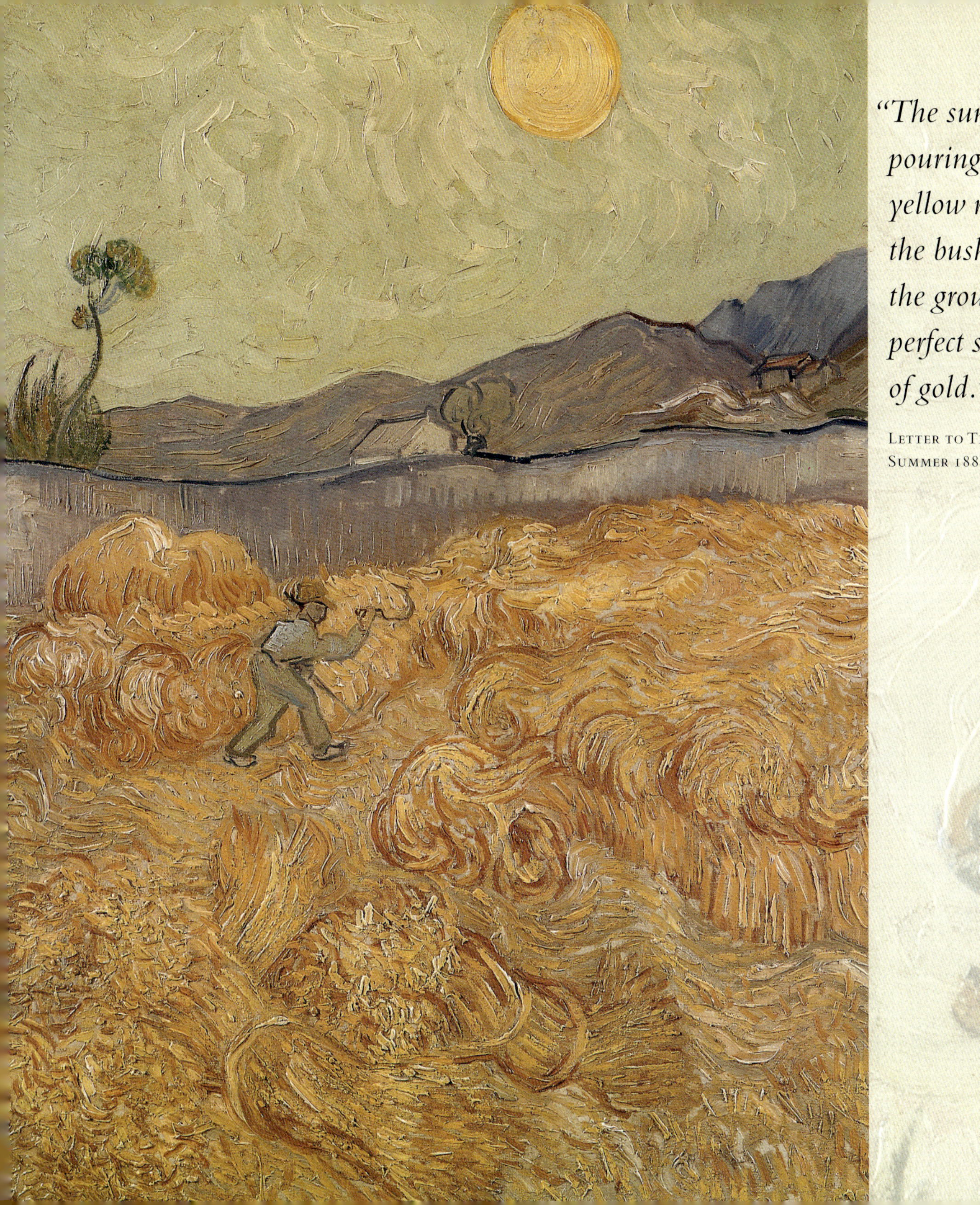

"The sun was pouring bright yellow rays on the bushes and the ground, a perfect shower of gold."

Letter to Theo,
Summer 1888

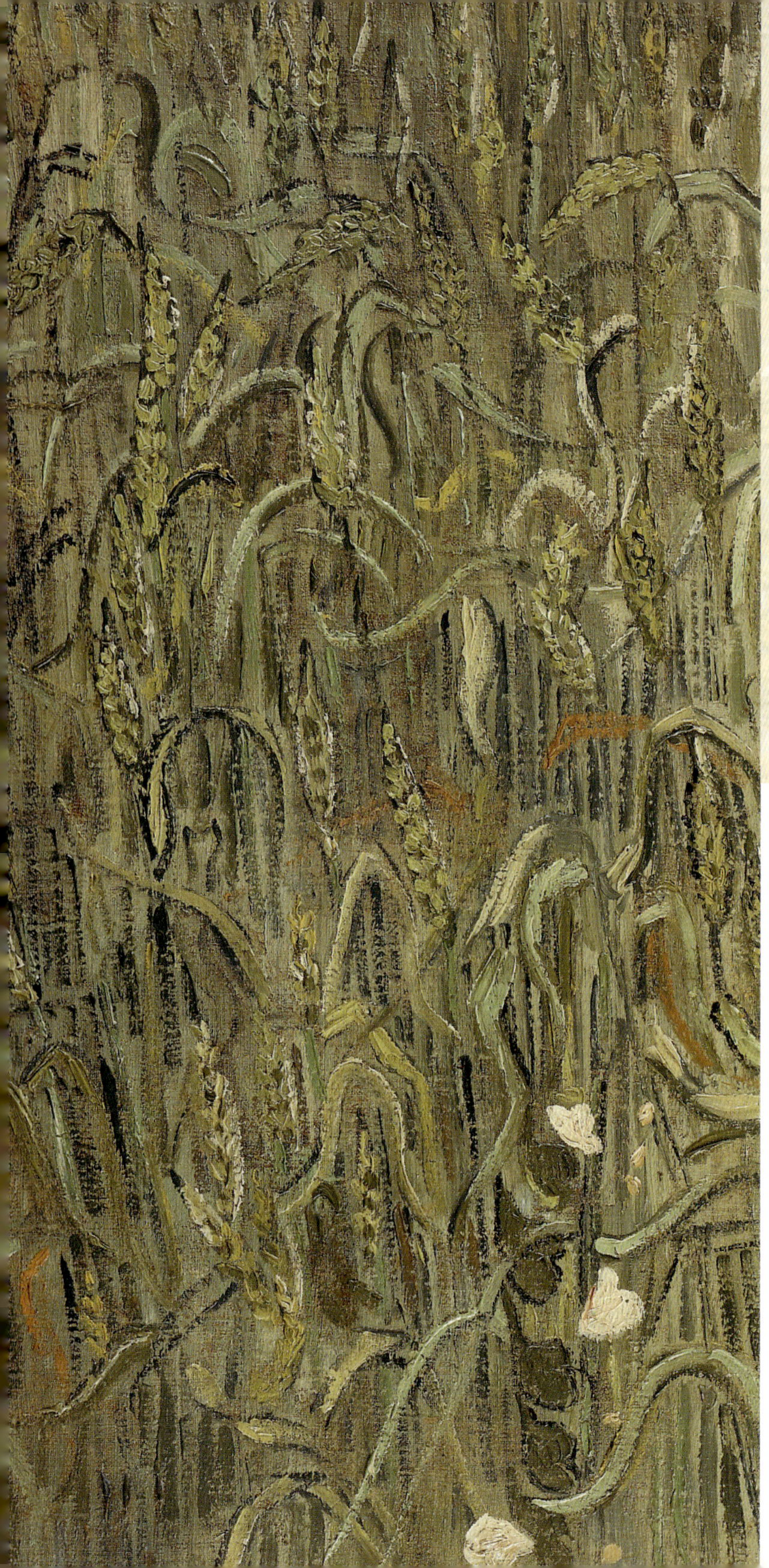

land, with well-defined plots, grain stacks, and the tools of labor, Vincent regarded it as an essential part of the landscape. The farmers appear as anonymous, almost incidental figures as they go about their work of reaping and hauling grain. He saw them as belonging to the ancient rhythm of life on the land.

When Vincent entered the hospital in Saint-Rémy in the early summer of 1889, he was convinced that the regular routine of the asylum would impose some order on his life. But, as he looked out to the fields beyond the village, he knew that painting in the open air was essential to restore his personal equilibrium. Just as he was always honest about his condition, he was patient with the doctors' restrictions. By mid-June, he was allowed to leave the hospital grounds. Accompanied by an attendant, he could go into the fields and paint. He wrote to Theo on June 25 that he had no news, that the days were all the same, and he had only one idea: "that a field of wheat or a cypress is well worth the trouble of looking at up close" (Letter 596).

As Vincent worked, his sense of self-reliance returned, and in a letter to his mother it is clear that by July 5, he was looking to life beyond the security of the asylum: "One never sees buckwheat or rape here, and perhaps there is in general less variety than with us. And I should so much like to paint a buckwheat field in flower, or the rape in bloom, or flax, but maybe I will have an opportunity for this later in Normandy or Brittany" (Letter 598).

Further attacks

By the middle of the month, Vincent was occupied with a painting of a reaper, swinging a sickle in a vast, rolling wheatfield. He was working on this when he had his first attack at Saint-Rémy. In a letter to Theo, he described the seizure in a matter-of-fact manner: "This new attack, my boy, came on me in the fields, on a windy day, when I was busy painting. I will send you the canvas, I finished it in spite of it" (Letter 601). But this latest attack was severe; the attendant with him claimed that during the seizure Vincent had attempted to eat his paint and drink his turpentine. Debilitated for more than five weeks, Vincent complained that his mind wandered, his swollen throat made it almost impossible to eat, and he was frequently tormented by disturbing dreams.

By early fall, Vincent's condition was stable and he fixed his energies on a single goal: to go out as much as possible and paint before the weather turned cold and grim. He confessed to Theo that he "felt like a fool going and asking doctors permission to make pictures," but he felt sure that "if sooner or later I get a certain amount better, it will be because I have recovered through working, for it is a thing which strengthens the will and consequently leaves those mental weaknesses less hold" (Letter 602).

A new element of discontent emerged in Vincent's letters; he complained about the food in the asylum and the expense, and he expressed a fear of the other patients. Theo began to investigate the possibility of bringing his brother to live under partial supervision in a village closer to Paris. He even approached a friend, the painter Camille Pissarro, asking if he would take Vincent to live in his home, but Pissarro was unable to help. He recommended instead that

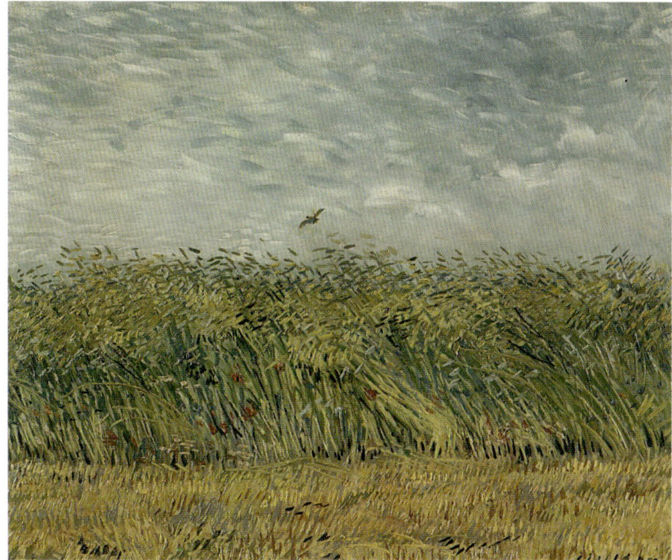

Vincent move to the town of Auvers-sur-Oise, where Paul Gachet, a physician and amateur artist, was willing to monitor his condition.

Meanwhile, despite his sense of confinement in the asylum, Vincent remained active and returned to his old practice of making copies of works he admired. Theo kept him supplied with prints, including reproductions of the works of Honoré Daumier, Delacroix, and Millet. Through his new interpretations of Millet's series *Labors of the Field*, Vincent reaffirmed his connection with nature. He painted all the types of toil in the series—threshing, cutting straw, sheepshearing, and digging—but two images provided

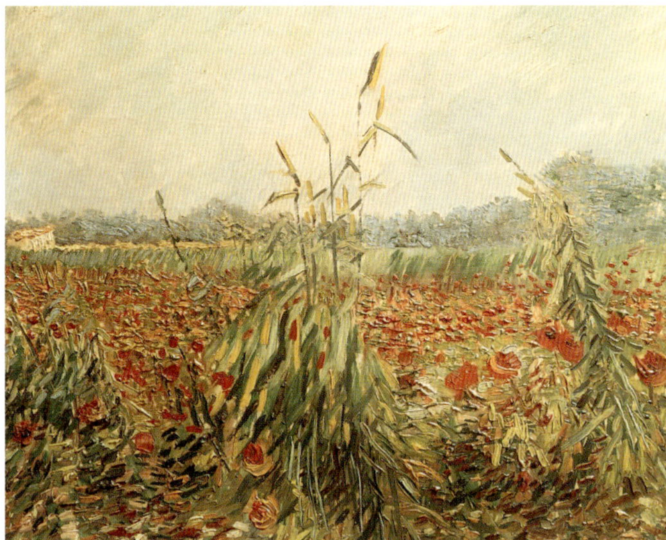

powerful counterpoints that defined the balance he sought in his life. One was the sower, which he had painted several times in Arles; the subject was inspired by Millet, but set within the new expressive forces of his own vision. The other was the reaper, which he was working on at the time of his most recent attack. Vincent took up the theme of the reaper again after his recovery. Its message, as he explained to Theo, was the opposite of that of the sower; rather than engendering new life, the reaper was "the image of death, in the sense that humanity might be what he is reaping" (Letter 604). But Vincent assured his brother, "there's nothing sad in this death, it goes its way in broad daylight with a sun flooding everything with a light of pure gold."

Vincent suffered another attack in December, but this time his recovery was rapid. Two more attacks occurred in January and February, requiring an extended convalescence. As he regained his strength, his desire to leave Saint-Rémy intensified, and by spring his condition was stable. As a voluntary patient, Vincent was free to discharge himself from the asylum at any time, and on May 16, 1890, he boarded a train for the journey north to Auvers-sur-Oise.

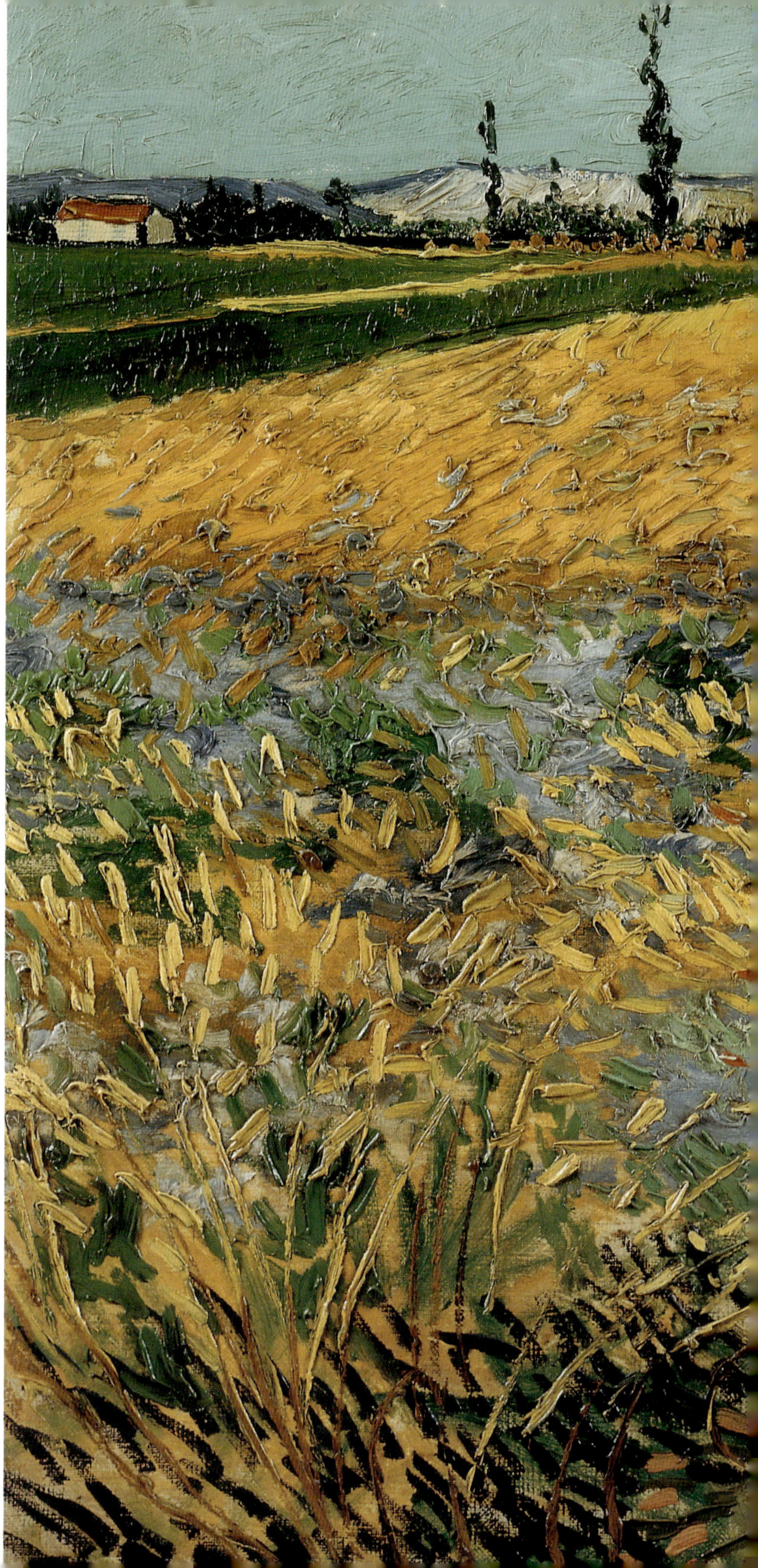

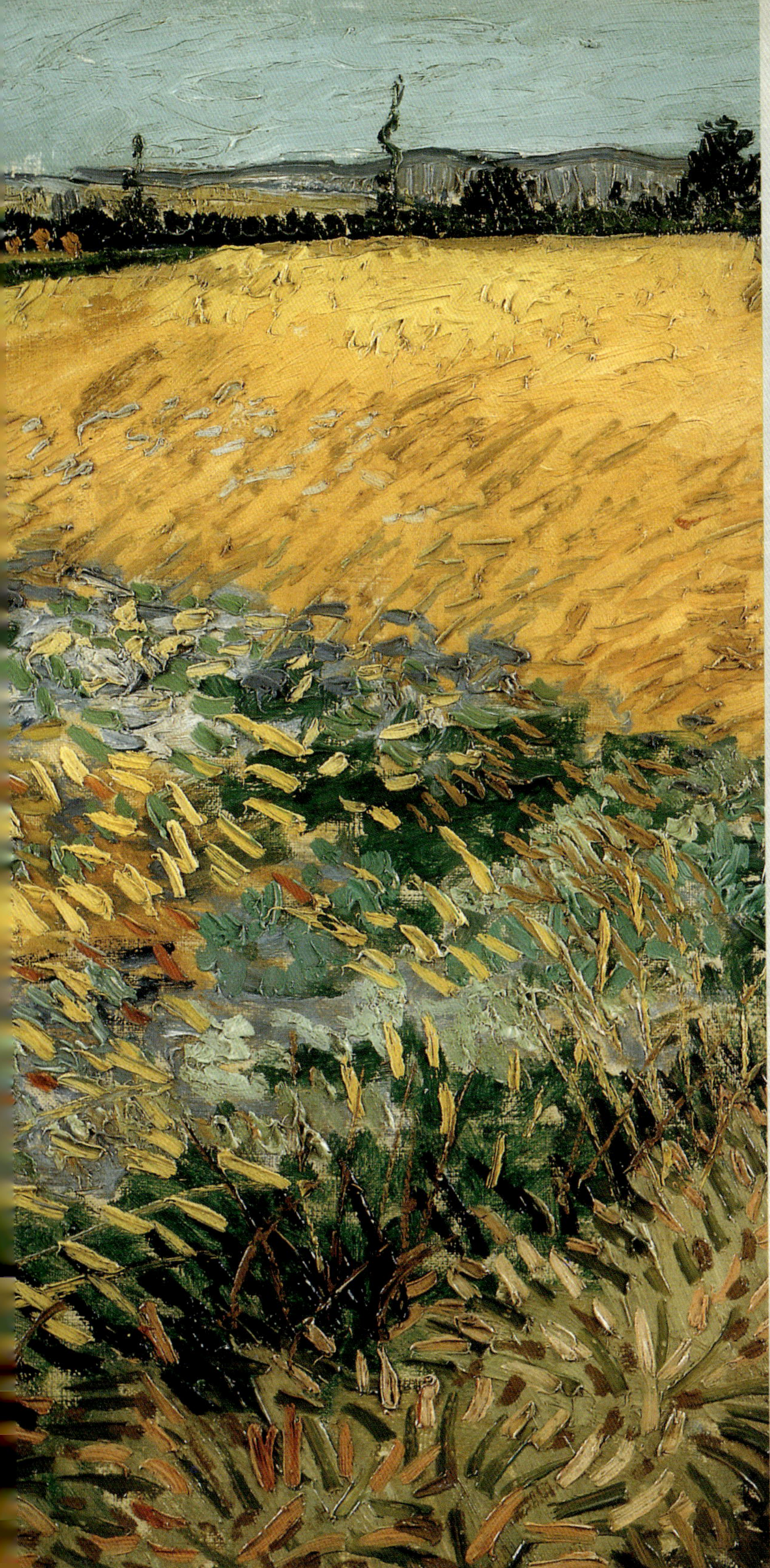

"One works better in the country; there everything speaks a distinct language, everything is firm, everything explains itself."

LETTER TO WIL, JANUARY 1890

Green Ears of Wheat FAR LEFT
JUNE 1888. THE ISRAEL MUSEUM, JERUSALEM

Although Vincent chose the naturalist technique of painting outside, his landscapes draw their power from the combination of observation and experience. In *Green Ears of Wheat*, he portrayed the view as it appeared before him—tall corn plants rising above a field of poppies with a stand of trees at the horizon, their leaves blue-green against the changing sky. But his application of paint heightens the expressive force. Long strokes of layered color make the corn stalks flutter, poppies nod beneath the weight of thick impasto, and the streaks of pale tone convey the movement of the clouds.

Wheatfield LEFT
JUNE 1888. VAN GOGH MUSEUM, AMSTERDAM

Wheatfield was painted at the same time as *The Harvest* and shares many of its visual and atmospheric elements. The view is vast, a spreading plain against a low horizon. Blunt hills roll in the distance. Only the sinuous forms of the randomly spaced trees break the band of the pale blue sky. The vivid tone and the absence of shadow in the painting assault the senses without relief, reflecting Vincent's compulsion to work under the blinding sun.

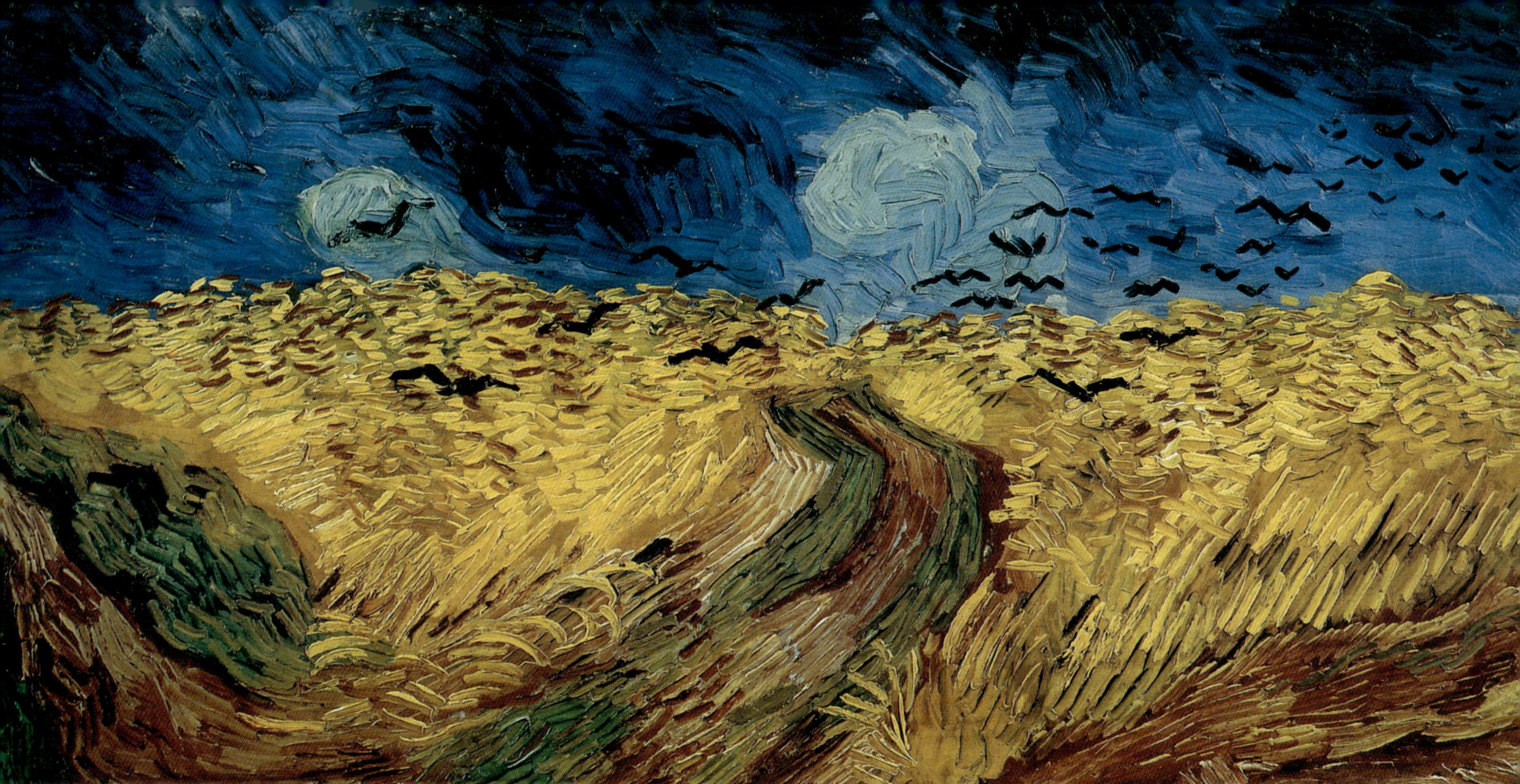

At his own insistence, he traveled alone, making a brief stop to see Theo and his family in Paris.

Upon Vincent's arrival in Auvers, he met Dr. Gachet, who found him accommodation at a local inn. Vincent liked the doctor immediately. An amateur artist and avid collector, Gachet took an active interest in Vincent's work, posing for portraits, allowing Vincent to paint his daughter and his home, and engaging him in lively discussions about art. Auvers also had a strong artistic tradition: Daumier, Corot, and Cézanne had all worked there at one time, and it had been the home of Charles-François Daubigny.

Vincent's first few letters from Auvers were cautiously optimistic. He wrote to Theo and and his wife Jo that he felt comfortable: "Here one is far enough from Paris for it to be the real country." He noted that the village had changed since Daubigny's time, but that even the "modern middle-class dwellings" were "very radiant and sunny and covered with flowers." Vincent was hopeful about his condition: "Up to now all is well. And it may yet improve, I still think that it is mostly a disease of the South that I have caught and that returning here will be enough to dissipate the whole thing" (Letter 637).

Vincent quickly adopted a regular routine. Every day he would leave the inn in the morning, taking his easel out to the countryside to spend the day painting. As he confided to his brother, the first rush of independent work unnerved him—"the brush almost slipped through my fingers"—but soon he was working with confidence, and he felt that the paintings were a testament to "the health and restorative forces that I see in the country" (Letter 649).

Through late June and July, Vincent's attention was concentrated on the wheatfields, which were rapidly ripening and would soon be harvested. He evoked the engaging power of the subject in a letter to his mother

The ominous mood of *Wheatfield with Crows* has long been interpreted as prophetic of Vincent's suicide. With its dramatic palette, writhing brush strokes, and tall wheat waving in a powerful wind, the painting has a mesmerizing turbulence. The rough paths hacked through the field seem to trail off into infinity and the circling crows echo the movement of the wheat below them. But if *Wheatfield with Crows* is viewed in the context of Vincent's faith in the natural course of life on the land, not as evidence of his psychological distress, the work takes on a richer meaning. The wheat is ripe, the summer storms are coming, and the crops must be harvested so the cycle can begin again. Vincent saw in the rhythms of the rural year a timeless accord of humanity with the natural world; through them, he affirmed his belief that he would find both inspiration for his art and purpose for his life in nature.

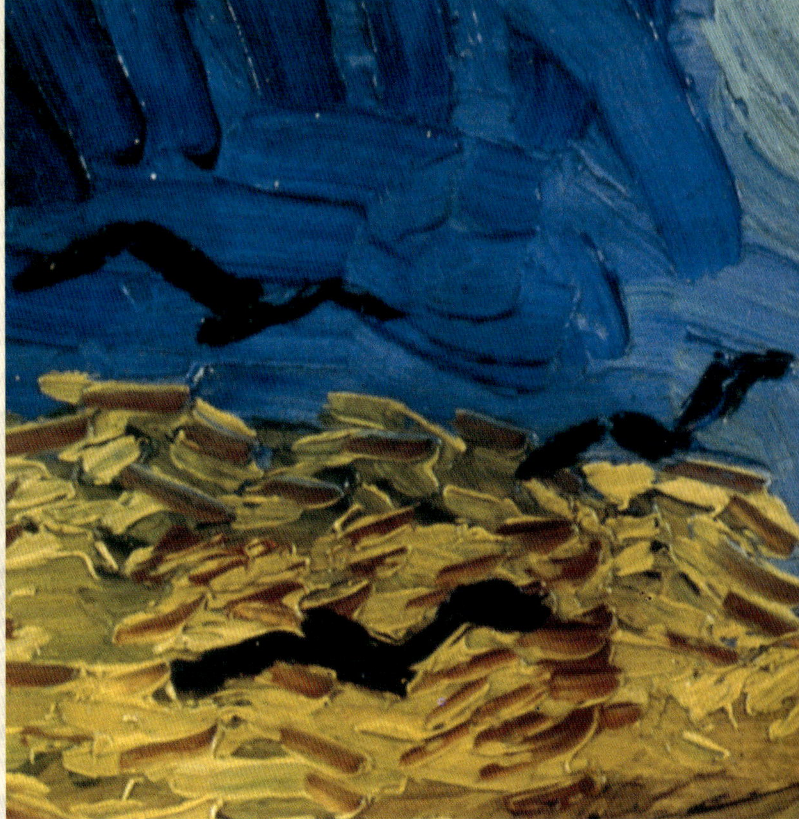

and his sister Wil, written on July 23: "I myself am quite absorbed in the immense plain with wheatfields against the hills, boundless as a sea, delicate yellow, delicate soft green, the delicate violet of a dug-up and weeded piece of soil, checkered at regular intervals with the green of flowering potato plants, everything under a sky of delicate blue, white, pink, violet tones" (Letter 650). His state of mind was in full accord with his natural subject; he told his mother and sister, "I am in a mood of almost too much calmness, in the mood to paint this."

Vincent painted *Wheatfield with Crows* in this broad cultivated plain. Although the picture cannot be dated precisely, Vincent was working on it during the final weeks of his life. In early July, he described the subject to Theo as "vast fields of wheat under troubled skies," and he wrote, "I did not need to go out of my way to try to express sadness and extreme loneliness" (Letter 649). In *Wheatfield with Crows* Vincent portrayed the natural cycle of life on the land. With thick, vibrant brush strokes, he painted the ripened wheat, blown by the winds of an impending summer storm. He captured the quick flight of the crows in a few stark strokes in black, as they circled low over the crops, under an ominous sky. Although Vincent ended his own life within weeks of painting this work, it would be wrong to regard it simply as prophetic of his suicide. As a painter of nature—of flowers and fields—Vincent observed the annual rhythms of the land. He welcomed the reaper as well as the sower, and *Wheatfield with Crows* speaks of acceptance rather than sorrow. As Vincent learned in the prospect of the harvest "there is nothing sad in this death."

Index

Author's Acknowledgments

In writing this book I had the generous encouragement and help of many people, and I would like to take the opportunity to thank them. The idea grew out of discussions with Caroline Bugler, and I am grateful to her for bringing the project into being. I thank my editor Jinny Johnson for her good humor and good work, and I thank Sarah Davies for matching the beauty of the paintings with the beauty of her design. At Frances Lincoln Limited, I want to express my appreciation to Anne Fraser and Ginny Surtees for guiding me throughout my endeavors, to Sue Gladstone for her unflagging efforts to get exactly the right pictures, and to Tom Armstrong and Tom Windross for their assistance. Thanks, as well, to Frances Lincoln for her gracious encouragement.

For assistance in my research, I would like to thank Roland Hansen and Josh Berta of the Flaxman Library at the School of the Art Institute of Chicago. I would also like to express my gratitude to the Newberry Library of Chicago for the support they give me as a Scholar-in-Residence. My parents, Elinor R. Mancoff and Philip Mancoff, also helped me with their enthusiasm and understanding, as well as their extraordinary ability to track down the books that were difficult to obtain. Finally, I want to acknowledge the interest of my cousin Ryan Plotsky, who shares my special regard for Vincent van Gogh and his art.

I can never look at flowers without remembering my uncle Isadore Mancoff's garden. As we walked through the tall plants, he would call my attention to each individual flower, holding his palm under the blossom, introducing me to his roses, his dahlias, and his bleeding hearts. My father Philip Mancoff still shares his brother's deep love and regard for growing things, and thanks to his patient labor and artistry, I have always lived with gardens. I am deeply grateful to my uncle and my father for teaching me to look closely at flowers and appreciate the beauty that human hands can cultivate but never quite reproduce. I dedicate this book to my father on the occasion of his eightieth birthday; his love of nature is as deep and life-affirming as that of Vincent van Gogh.

Debra N. Mancoff
Chicago, April 1999

Publisher's Acknowledgments

Editor: Jinny Johnson
Designer: Sarah Davies

Project Editor: Ginny Surtees
Art Editor: Anne Wilson
Picture Research: Sue Gladstone
Editorial Assistance: Tom Armstrong
Production: Hazel Kirkman

Frances Lincoln Publishers would also like to thank Melchert Zwetsman at the Van Gogh Musuem, Amsterdam for his help with this book, and Marie Lorimer for proofreading and supplying the index.

Photographic Acknowledgments

For permission to reproduce the paintings and archive photograph
on the following pages and for supplying photographs, the Publishers
thank those listed below.

AKG, London/Sotheby's New York: 7 and 50–51
Courtauld Institute, London/Bridgeman Art Library, London/New
York: 18
Israel Museum, Jerusalem/AKG, London (photo Erich Lessing): 86
LEFT
Collection Kröller-Müller Museum, Otterlo, The Netherlands: 4–5,
34, 35, 46, 47, 52, 53, 62–63
Kunsthalle, Bremen/Bridgeman Art Library, London/New York: 80
Kunsthaus, Zürich/Bridgeman Art Library, London/New York: 30
The Metropolitan Museum of Art : 57 (gift of Adele R. Levy, 1958.
58.187), photograph © 1985 The Metropolitan Museum of Art
The Museum of Modern Art, New York: 21 (acquired through the
Lillie P. Bliss Bequest), photograph © 1999 The Museum of Modern
Art, New York
National Gallery, London: 33, 66–67, 74
© 1999 Board of Trustees, National Gallery of Art, Washington: 24–
25 (gift of Pamela C. Harriman in memory of W. Averell Harriman),
76–77 (collection of Mr and Mrs Paul Mellon)
National Gallery of Canada, Ottawa: 32 (purchased 1951), 56
(purchased 1954)
National Gallery of Scotland: 44–45
Neue Pinakothek, Munich/AKG London: 72, 73
Oscar Reinhart Collection, Winterthur/Bridgeman Art Library,
London/New York: 19
Philadelphia Museum of Art: 70 (The Mr and Mrs Carroll S. Tyson,
Jr. Collection)
Van Gogh Museum, Amsterdam: 8–9, 10, 11, 12, 13, 14, 15, 22–23,
28, 29, 36, 37, 38–39 and back endpapers, 40, 41, 43, 48, 54, 55, 58,
59, 60, 64, 65, 68, 69, 71, 75, 78, 79, 81, 82, 83, 84, 85, 86–87 and
front endpapers, 88, 89
Wadsworth Atheneum, Hartford, Connecticut: 16 (gift of Philip L.
Goodwin in memory of his mother Josephine S. Goodwin), 27
(bequest of Anne Parrish Titzell)

*All works from the Van Gogh Museum, Amsterdam are on
permanent loan from the Vincent van Gogh Foundation

Selected Bibliography

Alpers, Svetlana, *The Art of Describing: Dutch Art in the Seventeenth
Century*. Chicago: University of Chicago Press, 1983

Bumpus, Judith, *Van Gogh's Flowers*. New York: Universe Books, 1989

The Complete Letters of Vincent van Gogh, 3 vols. Boston: New York
Graphic Society, 1958 (All quotes are taken from this source)

Hulsker, Jan, *The Complete Van Gogh: Paintings. Drawings. Sketches.*
New York: Harry N. Abrams, Inc., 1980

Japanese Prints Collected by Van Gogh. Exhibition Catalogue.
Amsterdam: Rijksmuseum, 1978

Kendall, Richard, *Van Gogh's Van Goghs: Masterpieces from the Van
Gogh Museum, Amsterdam*. Exhibition Catalogue. Washington, D.C.:
National Gallery of Art, 1998

Metzger, Rainer and Ingo F. Walther, *Vincent van Gogh 1853–1890*.
Cologne: Benedikt Taschen, 1996

McQuillan, Melissa. *Van Gogh*, London: Thames and Hudson, 1989

Pickvance, Ronald, *Van Gogh in Arles*. Exhibition Catalogue. New
York: The Metropolitan Museum of Art, 1987

Pickvance, Ronald, *Van Gogh in Saint-Remy and Auvers*. Exhibition
Catalogue. New York: The Metropolitan Museum of Art, 1987

Stein, Susan Alyson, *Van Gogh: A Retrospective*. New York: Hugh
Lauter Levin Associates, Inc., 1986

Sund, Judy, *True to Temperament: Van Gogh and French Naturalist
Literature*. Cambridge: University of Cambridge Press, 1992

Sweetman, David, *Van Gogh: His Life and His Art*. New York: Crown
Publishers, Inc., 1990

Uhde, W. *Van Gogh*, London: Phaidon Press, Ltd., 1995

Van Gogh, Elisabeth-du Quesne (trans. Katherine S. Dreier), *Personal
Reflections of Vincent van Gogh*. Boston: Houghton Mifflin Company,
1913

Walther, Ingo F. and Rainer Metzger, *Vincent van Gogh: The Complete
Paintings*. 2 vols. Cologne: Benedikt Taschen, 1990

Welsh-Ovcharov, Bogomila, *Van Gogh à Paris*. Exhibition Catalogue.
Paris: Editions de la reunion des musées nationaux, 1988

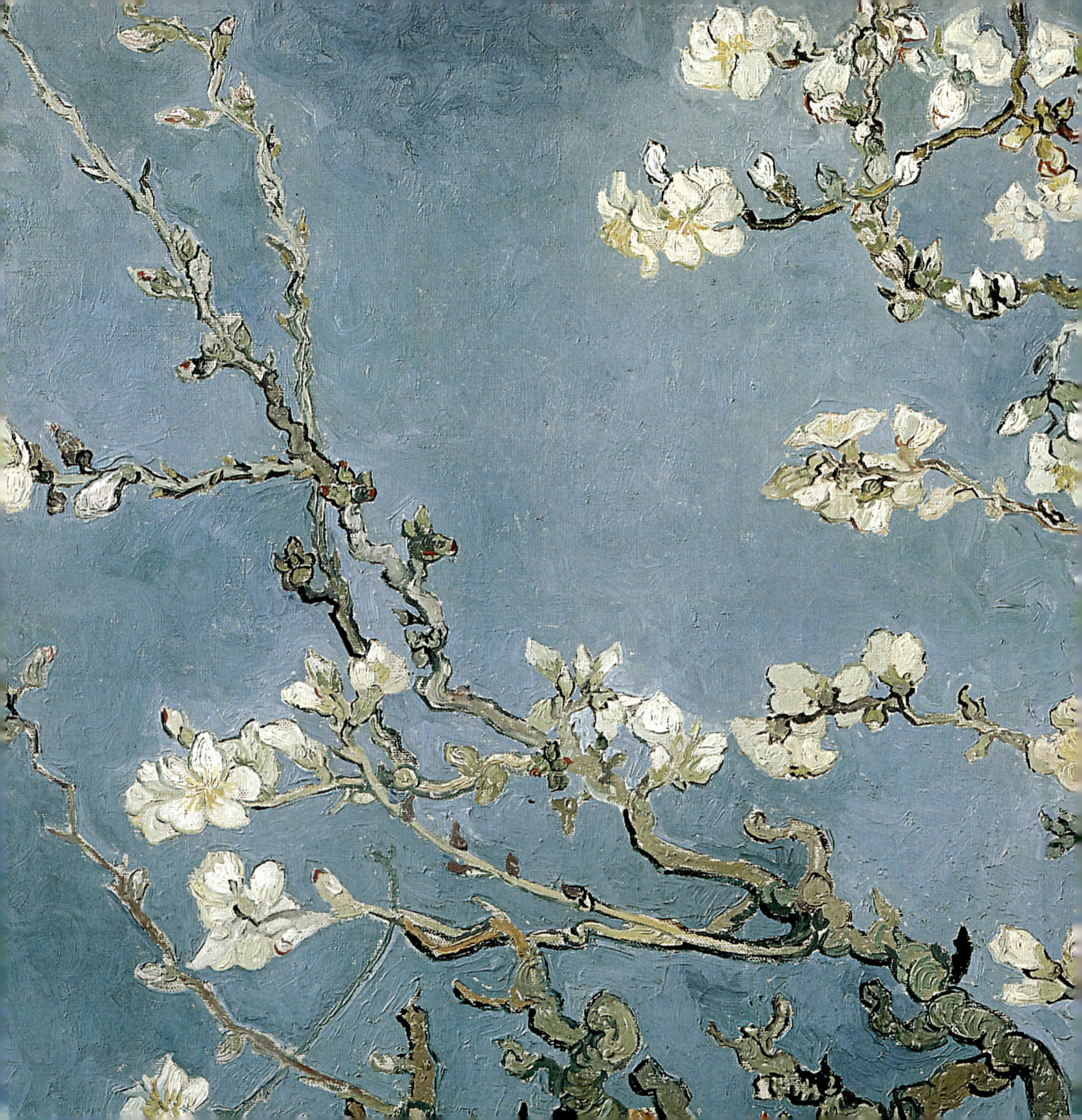